TruthQuest Student Commentaries

Up Close

with

Jesus

**getting deep
in the book
of Luke**

Steve Keels and Lawrence Kimbrough

UP CLOSE WITH JESUS
Getting Deep in the Book of Luke
Copyright © 2004 by Broadman & Holman Publishers
All rights reserved

Broadman & Holman Publishers
Nashville, Tennessee
broadmanholman.com

ISBN 0-8054-2852-6

Dewey Decimal Classification: 226.4
Subject Heading: Bible. N.T. Luke—Commentaries

Printed in the United States of America
1 2 3 4 07 06 05 04
EB

Oh, hi!

It's a good thing you stopped by when you did because we were just about to take off on a brand new Bible study: getting deep in the book of Luke and (much more importantly) getting way *Up Close with Jesus*.

So you couldn't have come by at a better time.

When you're studying Jesus' life, you just absolutely know that your own life will never be the same. Whether you're looking at His character and wanting to be more like Him, or you're standing there with your mouth wide open, amazed at what He's done for you—time spent with Jesus will leave you worshiping. His teaching will knock the legs out from under you one minute ("Whoever wants to save his life will lose it") and dust you off the next ("I have prayed for you, that your faith may not fail").

That's just the way He is. Incredible!

So while this book *is* a commentary—a chunk-by-chunk explanation of what the Bible says—it's much more than that. It's a way to deal honestly, regularly, repeatedly with the Word . . . and to let God change you from the inside out.

OK, let's go!

Real quick, let us give you a few tips and pointers on what to expect and how to make the most of this trip.

1] Pack your Bible. This book won't do you much good unless your Bible's right next to it. We're not going to be just retelling the stories and stuff. We're going to be commenting on them, helping you think about them and sort things out. So you'll need to know what the Bible says to make any sense of what we say.

2] Read ahead. You don't have to, but it wouldn't be the worst thing in the world if you'd go ahead and read the whole book of Luke first. That'll take you a couple of hours probably, but it'll be one of the best two hours you've ever spent. Reading a Bible book straight through really—really!—helps you understand it better. Even if you (hopefully) take time to do that, still be sure to read each individual Bible passage first before you read the commentary notes on it.

3] Look back. One of the most important things to know about the Bible is that it proves itself true. Only God could take dozens of writers, space them over thousands of years, and unite all their writings into one book that is totally consistent the whole way through. It's very important, then, to see what God was doing in all the different books of the Bible. So when you come to a place that asks you to look up a verse somewhere, be sure to do it. You'll get a lot more out of the trip that way.

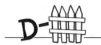

4] Be on the lookout. We've added several sidebars and other features to keep you from missing anything along the way. Here's what they'll look like. And here's what they'll do for you.

D-FENCE. This will highlight key verses or topics that are foundational to Christian living and thinking. They'll help you to be able to defend your faith better, to understand what others believe, and to make sharing Christ a more confident, productive experience.

DEFINITIONS. A lot of words used in the Bible—and the doctrinal terms that come from them—aren't all that easy to understand. Check here to get your fuzzy areas cleared up.

BIBLE REFERENCE. As often as possible, we'll dispatch you to another place in the Bible where you can see when an idea first shows up in the Scripture, or says something a different way, or gives you a better whole-Bible understanding. (Oh, and also, whenever you see a reference that just lists chapter and verse, like this—12:34, with no Bible book name—that means it's another passage from Luke.)

HISTORY. Part of what makes the Bible hard to interpret is that we don't always know the historical settings it was written in. These little side-notes will give you an idea of things the original Bible audience understood as common knowledge —the same way we understand things in our current culture.

MAPS. Every so often we'll drop in a map so you can see where you are.

TENSION. Some Bible verses—even after you've read them, and reread them, and read them some more—still don't seem to make any sense. Look for this in-text marker fairly often, where we'll do our best to help you wrestle with—and hopefully start to untangle—the toughest, knottiest passages. Sometimes we'll just have to leave it with a "we don't know for sure," but that's OK. If God's ways were always easy to understand, He wouldn't be much of a God, would He?

TRUTHQUEST QUESTIONS. We've also sprinkled in some room for you to write, to deal with some of the day-to-day implications of what you're reading in the Bible. Be sure not to skip over these or to settle for simple answers. These are important. The Bible is a living book.

5] Use this book as a devotional guide.

You can do this fairly easily by going one-by-one to the TruthQuest questions, using the passage where the question is found for your daily Bible reading, then praying or journaling your way through the answers. If nothing else, it'll give you something new to try—different from the usual devotional book or magazine—and it'll hold you for a month or so until God leads you to something else.

Who? What? Where?

Luke's Facts

- 24 chapters
- 1,151 verses
- around 24,000 words
- probably written in Rome around A.D. 60
- longest book in New Testament
- first in a two-part story—Acts is the sequel
- contains references to 31 Old Testament books

Luke's Bio

Luke was probably a doctor (Colossians 4:14), but we know he was a traveling companion of Paul, whose life story is a big part of the book of Acts, also written by Luke. Neither of the two books comes out and says that Luke is the author, but just about everybody from the second century on has accepted without question that this is Luke's Gospel—his account of Jesus' life. He was also the only one of the four Gospel writers who wasn't a Jew.

Luke's Book

This is a biography—a good one—but it's not intended to be complete, to track Jesus' life every waking moment. So a lot of the details are left out in order to communicate the bigger themes of Jesus' ministry and purpose. That's why it sometimes seems to skip from one event to the other.

Luke's Reasons

Luke explained in the first few verses that his book was written to a certain man named Theophilus (the-AHF-i-lus), who appeared to have had some exposure to Christianity. Perhaps he was already a Gentile (non-Jewish) believer, struggling with a faith and movement that was deeply rooted in the Jewish life and experience.

Luke's Big Outline

1:1–2:52 John the Baptist and Jesus
3:1–4:13 Jesus Gets Ready to Go
4:14–9:50 His Ministry in Galilee
9:51–19:44 His Journey to Jerusalem
19:45–24:53 His Final Days; His Parting Words

Luke's Big Ideas

HISTORICAL PROOF. Luke uses eyewitness accounts to show that Jesus was a real person who proved His claim that He was also the Son of God.
"Go and report to John the things you have seen and heard: The blind receive their sight, the lame walk, those with skin diseases are healed, the deaf hear, the dead are raised, and the poor have the good news preached to them" (7:22).

ISRAEL'S BAD LEADERSHIP. Over and over again in his slices-of-life stories from Jesus' everyday experiences, Luke shows how seriously the Jewish leaders had misunderstood God and misused His Word, turning His law into a weapon to control other people.
"Woe to you experts in the law! You have taken away the key of knowledge! You didn't go in yourselves, and you hindered those who were going in" (11:52).

ONE BIG TENT. Luke reveals that God had sent Jesus with some shocking news: those promises of His that were all about Israel? They're really for all of those who are becoming a part of His people—Jews and non-Jews (Gentiles) alike—through faith in the Son of God.
"Then the master told the slave, 'Go out into the highways and lanes and make them come in, so that my house may be filled'" (14:23).

RICH AND POOR. Not just the ones you'd expect will be swept into God's family. People from all walks of life—the good and the bad, the strong and the weak, the in-crowd and the unpopular—are all put on level ground in God's way of thinking.
"The Spirit of the Lord is on Me, because He has anointed Me to preach good news to the poor. He has sent Me to proclaim freedom to the captives and recovery of sight to the blind, to set free the oppressed" (4:18).

THE FINAL END. Luke is also very clear that there is coming a day when the saved will be rescued from their troubles, and the unsaved will find their troubles just beginning. Big pieces of Luke's Gospel are taken up with this life-and-death reality.
"You also be ready, because the Son of Man is coming at an hour that you do not expect" (12:40).

LESS IS MORE. Luke picks up on a lot of Jesus' teaching that deals with the high cost of servanthood, being a slave of Christ, pouring ourselves out in His service.
"For everyone who exalts himself will be humbled, and the one who humbles himself will be exalted" (14:11).

JESUS SAVES. There's basically one common thread that runs throughout the whole Bible: God will save His people. The four Gospels (the stories of Jesus' life), of course, make this really clear—Luke included.
"For the Son of Man has come to seek and to save the lost" (19:10).

Luke's Exclusives

There are a whole bunch of stories in Luke that you won't find in any of the other Gospels—Matthew, Mark, or John. Here are some of them:

- The birth of John the Baptist (1:5-25,57-80)
- Gabriel's visit to Mary (1:26-38)
- Mary's song (1:46-55)
- Joseph and Mary's trip to Bethlehem (2:1-7)
- The shepherds (2:8-20)
- Jesus' presentation in the temple as a baby (2:21-38)
- Jesus at 12—accidentally left behind in Jerusalem (2:41-50)
- Jesus' childhood and growing up years (2:40,52)
- Jesus reading the Scripture in His hometown church (4:16-30)
- Peter's big catch of fish (5:1-10)
- A widow's son raised from the dead (7:11-17)
- The 70-man (or 72-man) mission trip (10:1-3)
- The story of the good Samaritan (10:30-37)
- The story of the grouchy midnight neighbor (11:5-8)
- Challenging the Jewish leaders (11:37-53)
- The story of the "build bigger barns" rich fool (12:13-21)
- The story of the unproductive fig tree (13:6-9)
- Healing a crippled woman on the Sabbath (13:10-17)
- Jesus' weeping over Jerusalem's fate (13:34-35; 19:41-44)
- The high cost of discipleship (14:28-33)
- The story of the lost sheep (15:1-7)
- The story of the lost coin (15:8-10)
- The story of the lost son (15:11-32)
- The story of the dishonest manager (16:1-11)
- The story of the rich man and Lazarus (16:19-31)
- Healing ten lepers—and only one said thanks (17:11-19)
- The story of the persistent widow (18:1-8)
- The story of the hypocrite and the humble pray-er (18:9-14)
- Zacchaeus—that wee little man (19:1-10)
- The second phase of Jesus' trial—before Herod (23:6-12)
- The resurrected Jesus on the road to Emmaus (24:13-35)

Luke 1

1:1-4 Prologue

The Gospel Writers' Club (verses 1-2)

Gabriel visits Mary — Nazareth — Capernaum — Sea of Galilee — MEDITERRANEAN SEA — SAMARIA — Jordan River — Gabriel visits Zacariah — Jerusalem — Bethlehem — DEAD SEA

You might have thought Matthew, Mark, Luke, and John were the only four biographies ever written about Jesus. But, nope. There were others already in circulation when Luke put his together. Verse 1, in fact, comes right out and says that Luke wasn't the first to write about who Jesus is and what He did during His earthly life. Most likely, though, many of these other writings weren't complete accounts. A lot of them probably focused on just one or two aspects, like Jesus' crucifixion or His resurrection.

A Reason for Writing (verses 3-4)

Luke also was well aware that no one could ever cover all the things Jesus did and said. Like other Gospel writers, he had to be selective in what he recorded. Not everything he turned up in his reading, memories, and interviews would become part of his account, but only what met with his purpose: helping his reader know that what was being reported about Jesus was true . . . and could stand the test of authentic historical research.

1:5-25 John the Baptist Is Coming

ANGELS.
Gabriel, one of the few angels whose name is ever told to us, appears four times in the Bible —twice to Daniel and twice in this one chapter. Unlike the TV and movie myths, real angels are created beings who serve God and carry out His will, not dead people reincarnated .

Usually when you hear that someone's going to have a baby, it's a young married couple (not always so young, but y'know—twenties, thirties, maybe forties). It's a really exciting time, as you'll probably get to find out one of these days. The two birth announcements in this chapter, though, are NOT normal.

The first came to a really old couple, Zechariah and Elizabeth, who were way past their family-raising days. But they were "righteous in God's sight, living without blame"—which probably meant there were many people in Israel who weren't and didn't. It wasn't unusual, then, to catch Zechariah in the very act of obedience—like he is seen here, performing his priestly duty, burning incense in the temple. This practice dated back to the original giving of the law (see Exodus 30:1-10,34-38) and was still being followed by those who—like Zechariah—were descendants of the early priests (1 Chronicles 24).

So the angel Gabriel announced that Zechariah and Elizabeth were going to become the parents of a prophet—wow—at *their* age! And the old priest responded with a question (wouldn't you?) much like his forefather Abram (later known as Abraham) had asked in similar circumstances (see Genesis 15:8). Yet, Zechariah apparently lacked—on some level—the depth of genuine faith Abram possessed, for even though the two men's words were almost identical (compare them yourself), God wasn't happy with Zechariah. He even made him unable to speak until the words of this prophecy came to pass.

CHOSEN BY LOT.
Not sure exactly what this ancient practice looked like, but it amounted to a roll of the dice. The outcome was understood to be controlled by God and was used in determining His will (see Proverbs 16:33).

Verse 17. How can God already declare what John will be like . . . before John is even born . . . before he's taken his first step or made his first conscious decision? What if this guy doesn't want to be a prophet when he grows up? Doesn't he get to have any say at all? Yet somehow, in the mystery of God's knowledge and wisdom, His plan for our lives can be set in stone without trampling on our own free will. It elevates *Him* without diminishing *us*.

1:26-38 Jesus' Birth Is Announced

Fast forward six months, and Gabriel appeared again to deliver the second birth announcement, this time to a young virgin girl named Mary. Can you imagine an angel showing up in your room one day—and then giving you a shocker like this? I mean, she was just an ordinary girl. Just . . . Mary. Never-done-anything-to-get-pregnant Mary.

VIRGIN BIRTH.
The basis for this central truth of Christian doctrine lies here, as well as in Matthew 1:18-25. Jesus was miraculously conceived, with no human father, in fulfillment of Isaiah 7:14. To believe otherwise is to doubt the Word of God.

SALVATION.
Look back to Jeremiah 23:5-6, and see how closely Zechariah's song resembles this early prophecy—now coming into fulfillment before his very eyes.

Just like his prophecy to Zechariah had been, Gabriel's whole idea seemed impossible, and Mary's response exposed her honest inability to understand. But rather than being reprimanded, she received God's patience and encouragement. Her "how can this be?" (verse 34) differs slightly yet significantly from Zechariah's "how can I know this?" (verse 18). Think about it.

The connection between these two accounts is further deepened by the fact that Elizabeth, the now-expecting mother of John the Baptist, was a relative of hers. This gave Mary someone to confide in.

 Mary was "deeply troubled" by hearing Gabriel pay her the compliment of being favored by God (verses 28-29). But you'd think she'd be happy about it. What is "troubling" about God's pleasure?

_____

_____

_____

_____

1:39-56 John and Jesus, Together

Elizabeth's Prophecy (verses 39-45)

ABORTION.
One of the Bible's greatest defenses of the unborn child is this account of John recognizing Jesus in utero [verse 41].

Likely seeking an understanding ear to share her secret with, Mary hurried to the home of Elizabeth, whose unborn child did some sort of back flip inside of her . . . simply because Jesus was in the room. Already, these two sons were seen in their proper relationship—Jesus, superior to John.

Elizabeth's words in verse 42, like Gabriel's in verse 28, were used in later centuries to exalt Mary to divine-like status. Some still believe this today. But this misses the point—not only the point of these passages but also of the whole New Testament. Mary was the *recipient* of grace, not a *source* of grace. She was blessed, not by being divine or godlike, but by becoming a willing channel of God's blessing to others.

Mary's Song (verses 46-56)

Mary responded to Elizabeth's words and her own growing awe at this heavenly miracle with a hymnlike poem, often called the *Magnificat.*

Verse 48. How could a sinful woman be the mother of the Son of God? How could Jesus share Mary's human genes yet still be divine? First Corinthians 15 helps us out here. Verse 22 of that chapter says all of us (Mary included) were born under the curse of death by virtue of our common ancestor, Adam. But even though Jesus' mother was born a sinner, Jesus' heavenly Father was not. Therefore, Jesus was not a fallen man. He wasn't born with the built-in guilt of inherited sin like we are. Jesus was the new Adam (1 Corinthians 15:45), whose sinless heritage overrode His mother's fallenness.

1:57-80 The Birth of John the Baptist

What to Name the Baby? (verses 57-66)

When you're about to have a baby, it's really hard to narrow all the names you like down to one. Sure, there are some names you just don't like. But choosing just one when you like about three or four—it's tough! It was especially hard for Zechariah and Elizabeth, whose neighbors and relatives were all expecting them to name their son Zechariah Junior, after his daddy. The angel had told them, though, to name him John; remember verse 13? And remember how obedient these two were said to have been? So John it was—no matter what everybody else said.

A New Day Is Dawning (verses 67-79)

Whew—what a relief! It had been nine months since Zechariah had spoken a single word. (Imagine going that long without talking on your cell phone!) And now with his speech restored to him—as promised (verse 20)—Zechariah was filled with the Spirit, prophesying about the

NAMING.
You may wonder why this event caused such an uproar. The biblical concept of naming children was rooted in the ancient world's understanding that a given name expressed a person's essence. This was simply a much more serious matter than we know it today.

COVENANT.
Biblical covenants were binding agreements initiated by God between Him and His people. "If you...then I." The word testament is a synonym for covenant. So the Old and New Testaments tell about God's covenant with Israel and His covenant with those who come to Him by faith in His Son Jesus Christ.

HOUSE OF DAVID.
David was the greatest king ever in Israel, but prophecy revealed that an even greater ruler would one day come from his line. Read Jeremiah 33:17-26. And don't miss Isaiah 9:6-7.

faithfulness of God and about the new era, which is set to arrive, concerning God's covenant with His people. Zechariah's song is often called the *Benedictus*, with the first half (verses 68-75) weaving together several Old Testament promises that were finally ready to come to pass.

Out in the Wilderness (verse 80)

Luke summed up John's childhood in a single verse that left a waiting world breathless. Yes, John had been dispatched into the wilderness for this time. But one day in his rugged home-away-from-home, he heard God's call. He then came back into public view with an urgent call to repentance ... and an amazing announcement of the soon-and-coming Messiah.

What do you think Zechariah's nine months of silence were like to him? What would nearly a year without talking do to you? Would it make you more submitted to God or more sorry for yourself?

_____

_____

_____

_____

Luke 2

CENSUS.
Governments still do these population counts today to gather statistics and help their planning decisions. In Bible times these were usually conducted for collecting taxes or determining manpower for war.

2:1-20 The Birth of Jesus

A Part of History (verses 1-7)

Luke's approach to this story shows two important things: First, by placing Jesus' birth in the context of world events—when Caesar Augustus was ruler of the Roman Empire—he's saying that God was working in real time and through the decisions of ongoing national politics to perform His will. The emperor thought he was just ordering a population census, but God was actually using him to orchestrate history for His own purposes.

Which brings us to point two: Jesus' being born not at home in Nazareth but in Bethlehem shows Him to be the coming king who had been promised by the prophets (check out Micah 5:2).

Heaven Touches Earth (verses 8-14)

You know how people pay attention when there's a big announcement to make at school? Or when they're announcing a major storm warning on TV or the winners of an award contest? But nothing compares to the drama of this announcement: angels gathering around a bunch of shepherds on an ordinary hillside the night of Jesus' birth.

Verse 11 tells them (and us) about who this Jesus is. Each of the three titles—Savior, Christ, and Lord—has significant meaning (see SAVIOR sidebar).

Verse 14. This has been translated various ways, but the most accurate seems to be, not the famous King James, Christmas carol refrain of "peace, good will toward men," but rather "peace on earth to people He favors." Does this mean, then, that for some people, Jesus' coming didn't bring the promise of peace? Does He "favor" some and not "favor" others? Maybe a better question to ask is why He "favors" any of us at all. Certainly, the message of the gospel is for everyone, but not everyone will receive His salvation—His favor.

The Shepherds' Story (verses 15-20)

The shepherds were not only the first to hear the proclamation of the good news but also the first to tell others. Makes you wonder if we're as eager to tell the story of what we've seen and heard.

SAVIOR.
This means one who delivers from danger, one who heals. [See Isaiah 43:1-13, especially verses 3 and 11.] CHRIST means "anointed" and is nearly synonymous with MESSIAH, "the anointed one," meaning that the power of God was upon Him. LORD, meaning one who has power, shows that Jesus was not just a man but truly God Himself. These three titles also appear together in Philippians 3:20.

THE LAW.
More than just the Ten Commandments. It's all the ceremonial and civil duties that are written about in the first five books of the Bible, also known as the PENTATEUCH [PEN-tuh-tuke] or, in Jewish terms, the Torah.

BABY CEREMONIES.
All three of the rites for new-borns performed by Mary and Jesus came straight from the Old Testament: CIRCUMCISION, or removing a fold of skin from the male organ, PURIFICATION after childbirth, and the BURNT OFFER-ING to be presented about a month later. See it all spelled out in Leviticus 12:2-8.

2:21-39 Jesus as a Baby

According to the Law (verses 21-24)

It's clear that God had entrusted His Son to an earthly couple who were devout in their religious faith and practice. Five times throughout this passage (verses 22,23,24,27,39), Luke mentions that Mary and Joseph acted according to the law. If God was going to place His Son in a human family, that's what you'd expect, right?

But would you expect Him to give Jesus to a man and wife who were this poor—like the people who drive up in run-down cars or go around in worn-out clothes? That's kind of how Mary and Joseph showed up at the temple. They were compelled by command and conscience to bring an offering of sacrifice there for their newborn son. But the offering they brought (either a pair of doves or pigeons) pegged them as being from poor families (see Leviticus 12:8). They were pictures of God's mercy on public display.

What lesson is God teaching us by allowing His Son to be born in a stable instead of a high-class hotel, or for His parents to have to bring a couple of cheap birds to the altar rather than the customary lamb?

_____

_____

_____

_____

GENTILES.
These are people who are not part of God's chosen family at birth. In the biblical context, this basically means non-Jews, sometimes called other ugly names like pagans or heathens.

The Shadow of the Cross (verses 25-39)

Think of a Christian teacher you know—either at school or at church—someone who has a lot of wisdom, who pays close attention to what God says, someone you really respect. That's Simeon, a devout man living in Jerusalem at the time of Jesus' birth. Truly, God had revealed a clear message to this faithful servant: Simeon would see the Messiah with his own eyes, and Jesus would not be coming only for those in the nation of Israel but for people all over the world (see Isaiah 49:6). The prophetess Anna recognized this too.

Simeon warned that Jesus would cause both the "fall" and "rise" of many in Israel, and that although Mary was certainly blessed in being the mother of God's Son, her close relationship to Jesus would also result in "a sword" of worry, sadness, and pain. This was the first connection in Luke between Jesus' mission and His suffering. Already, the shadow of the cross was falling across His life. He is the salvation of God—*yay!*—but in the midst of such hope lived the chilling reality that ultimate victory would not come without a huge cost.

2:40-52 Jesus as a Boy

It's almost hard to believe, but Jesus was at one time a junior high boy. Wow. How would you have liked being in His class or sitting next to Him on exam day? Imagine what it would have been like having Him for a big brother. Quite an act to follow, huh?

Well, apart from the summary statements about Jesus' growth in verses 40 and 52, our only knowledge of Jesus' childhood comes from this episode of Jesus in the temple. This brief glimpse of Jesus as a child forms a kind of bridge between the events connected with His birth and the account of His adult ministry to come, revealing the clear direction God was already taking with His Son.

After this, Jesus dutifully returned to Nazareth with His parents, where He grew intellectually ("in wisdom"), physically ("in stature"), spiritually ("in favor with God"), and socially ("in favor with people").

PASSOVER.

Passover was one of three annual festivals that Jewish men of Jesus' day were required to celebrate in Jerusalem (find all of these events listed in Deuteronomy 16:1-17). Passover is the opening feast of the seven-day festival called the Feast of Unleavened Bread, commemorating God's deliverance of His people from slavery (see Exodus 12)—when death came to all the firstborn of the Egyptians but "passed over" the people of Israel.

Verse 40 (and 52). Jesus was God, right? Eternal, unchanging, all-everything God. So why did He have a need to grow and develop, to get sore muscles, to learn how to act in public, to go through puberty? It is because He also possessed the full nature of our humanity …and had to identify with us on every level in order to take our place as a sinless sacrifice (see Hebrews 5:8-9).

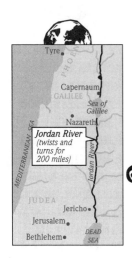

Verse 49. Was Jesus just acting up here? Smarting off to His mother? Disobeying the direct command of His worried parents? It sort of looks like it, but (of course) He wasn't. Remember that unlike most situations where a child has been adopted, Jesus' real Father was still involved in His life. Jesus wasn't just in the temple that day; He was truly in His Father's house, obeying Him above every other authority.

Think of a twelve-year-old you know—or of yourself when you were twelve? How does Jesus' maturity at such a young age compare to your own experience? Why do you think He already knew so much?

_____

_____

_____

Luke 3

3:1-6 John the Baptist Returns

JOHN'S PROPHECY.
Verses 4-6 come from Isaiah 40:3-5—another connection with Old Testament prophecy — and also a declaration that John's message of repentance and the coming of Christ would put everyone on level ground before God.

Everything in the first verse and a half is—again, as we saw at the beginning of chapter 2—helping Luke's reader place Jesus on the timeline of history. Luke was writing his Gospel about a Savior for all the people, and he wanted his old pal Theophilus to see that these events were part of a real world shared by Jews and Gentiles alike.

Now—have you ever been in a situation where you knew you had to tell the truth, but you also knew it was going to make you really unpopular? That'll help you see what John the Baptist was up against. Starting with the second half of verse 2, Luke picks up the story of John, whom we left at the end of chapter 1 living in the wilderness and waiting on God's timing to go public with his ministry. At this time he was fully in action, "preaching a baptism of repentance for the forgiveness of sins." Many of the Old Testament prophets used various kinds of symbols in their preaching; John's prophetic sign was baptism. It communicated visually what repentance did in people's hearts.

3:7-20 John's Message and Mission

Baptism and Repentance (verses 7-9)
John showed a willingness to be brutally honest, untactfully truthful. (Luke said, "Brood of vipers!" meaning people who are in Satan's grip.) He knew that many of the people were coming to him only for the outward sign of baptism but with no intention of repentance. They had no desire to depend on anything other than their family name and heritage.

A Whole New Way of Life (verses 10-14)
Some who came to John, however, were seriously wanting to change. People who'd been addicted to drugs or alcohol or pornography, people who'd made real messes of their lives, did not enjoy the end results of the situations they found themselves in. They didn't know how, but they wanted to be different. And these were the types of folks who were begging John to help them change.

In many cases they were the least liked, the least respected, the last people on earth who the self-righteous and privileged expected to see. John's answers to their sincere "What should we do?" questions revealed that a truly repentant person is not just happy that God has treated him with mercy and compassion. A genuinely changed person also wants to treat others with the same kind of sacrificial love.

The Spirit and Fire (verses 15-20)
Because John's activity aroused great religious interest and speculation, it was only natural that some in Israel would wonder if John was the Messiah. He quickly denied this.

He had other things on his mind—like feeling forced

REPENTANCE.
More than being sorry, repentance is the next logical step of action —a complete change of mind, a noticeable, consistent turning away from sin and heading in the direction of righteousness.

TAX COLLECTORS.
These government agents of Rome were responsible for gathering tax money from people in their provinces. They often inflated the amount that was owed and pocketed the difference.

SOLDIERS.
These were members of the military, of course, but not of an Israelite army. These were Roman soldiers who enforced the peace in regions that were under Roman occupation, as in Judea.

WINNOWING.
The process of shoveling grain into the air, allowing the wind to blow off the fly-away straw, while the heavier, pure grain was separated for use.

to speak out on a current issue that was so immoral he just couldn't keep quiet about it. John's problem with Herod the tetrarch (verses 19-20), the current governor of the area and son of King Herod, was that he had divorced his wife and taken his *brother's* wife for his own. This appeal for morality in public office would eventually cost John his life (Matthew 14:1-12).

Why would John be so adamant about bringing baptism to the most ungodly people on earth? How do you view men and women—or people your age that you know—who live a very corrupt lifestyle?

_____
_____
_____

Verse 16. What did John mean about Jesus' baptizing us with "the Holy Spirit and fire"? Is this something different than water baptism? Something more than Christian conversion? This seems to refer to the Holy Spirit's dramatic appearance following Jesus' return to heaven (Acts 1:5), most vividly seen on the day of Pentecost (Acts 2:1-13). Since Luke was also the writer of Acts, he was very aware—perhaps an eyewitness by the time of this writing—of the power of these phenomenal first-century events.

3:21-22 Jesus' Baptism

Have you ever been at church when a whole bunch of people were being baptized at once? Luke's account of Jesus' baptism emphasizes that it happened like that—when all the people were being baptized. This shows Jesus' intent to identify with those He had come to serve and to save.

Verse 21. Why did Jesus have to be baptized? Was He guilty of sin? Needing to repent? In Matthew's Gospel, John sort of balks at this idea too, but Jesus told him to go ahead, "because this is the way for us to fulfill all righteousness" (Matthew 3:15). Jesus was acknowledging that the standard of life John was demanding of others was also true for Him. He was setting an example of obedience for us to follow.

3:23-28 Jesus' Family Tree

This genealogy is—again—a nod to Jesus' link in human history, much like the one that appears in Matthew 1:1-17. The most telling phrase in the whole passage is that Jesus was the "son of Adam, son of God" . . . and ready to begin the most important ministry humankind had ever known.

THE TRINITY.
In this spectacular scene, all three members of the Trinity appear at once: the SPIRIT descending from heaven in the form of a dove, the SON— Jesus —and the FATHER, echoing words of blessing from Psalm 2:7 and Isaiah 42:1. Yes, they are one complete whole, yet three distinct persons.

Luke 4

4:1-13 Jesus Is Tempted

The book of James says that sin is so much a part of us, we can be tempted all by ourselves without the Devil even showing up (James 1:14). But not Jesus. There was no sin in Him at all, so it was up to the Devil to present Him three ways to scratch the basic itches common to all humanity, which are spelled out in 1 John 2:16: "the lust of the flesh" (the desire for physical satisfaction), "the lust of the eyes" (the hunger for power), "and the pride in one's lifestyle" (the allure of fame and recognition).

Jesus didn't have to give in to each of these sins in order to identify with what we go through in life, but He did have to be "tested in every way as we are" (Hebrews 4:15).

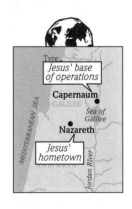

Tyre

Jesus' base of operations

Capernaum

GALILEE

MEDITERRANEAN SEA

Sea of Galilee

Nazareth

Jesus' hometown

Jordan River

WILDERNESS.
In Bible regions, these were typically dry, fearful wastelands with little rain and no people, known more for their harsh, rocky terrain than as endless expanses of white-hot sand dunes.

And are we ever! We're tempted to be sexually immoral, greedy, self-absorbed, arrogant. But by facing these temptations without sinning, Jesus actually showed Himself to be more human than we are, for sin has caused us to fall beneath our dignity. The sinless Christ is a picture of what humankind was originally created to be.

Notice how Jesus used Scripture each time to battle the Devil's temptations. If you want to see where His answers come from, visit Deuteronomy 8:3, 6:13, and 6:16.

Verse 1. You'd think the Holy Spirit would lead Jesus away from temptation, not directly into the wilderness for that very purpose. In fact, Jesus would later teach us in the Lord's Prayer to ask God regularly to "lead us not into temptation." Certainly, the Bible comforts us with the knowledge that we will never be faced with more temptation than we can bear (1 Corinthians 10:13), but it also confronts us with the reality that we need to face temptation in order to build the muscles of endurance (James 1:2-4).

Verse 2. Listen to this statement: "God is not tempted by evil" (James 1:13). Hmm. Then why in the world are we reading this story of Jesus—who was every bit God—being tempted by the Devil . . . if that's not even possible? Luke continues to show us a Jesus who is as human as He is divine. Jesus the Son of God cannot be tempted. But Jesus the son of Mary can be tempted, or He is not really a man.

SYNAGOGUE.
This was the local meeting and assembly place for the Jewish people, close to what we'd think of as a church building.

4:14-30 Jesus Ministers in Galilee

Starting Out (verses 14-15)
Luke begins his portrayal of Jesus' ministry by describing Him as being filled with "the power of the Spirit," fully equipped for these years of high acclaim and bitter accusation.

Jesus' Mission Statement (verses 16-21)

Many expected the Messiah to fulfill this passage from Isaiah 61:1-2 in nothing more than a physical sense—by restoring Israel to its former (or even greater) glory. But Jesus had come to lift the weight of spiritual captivity, spiritual blindness, spiritual oppression. Truly—in the deepest sense of these words—the Scripture was being fulfilled in Him.

SABBATH.
This day of rest and worship was observed on the seventh day of the week. It was a command of God (Exodus 20:8-11) that not only referred to God's resting on the seventh day of creation but also provided a preview of the eternal rest promised to God's people.

How did Jesus describe His mission? How specific was He in expressing what He had been placed on the earth to do? How would you describe God's mission for you? Could you put it into words, on paper?

Hometown Rejection (verses 22-30)

You know what it's like when you go to a family reunion, and even though you're older than you were before, everyone still treats you like you're a little kid, like you've never changed? When Jesus went home to Nazareth, they just couldn't accept the fact that He was anything more than Joseph and Mary's little boy.

Sure, they were glad to see He was doing well for Himself. They were impressed by His presence, His abilities. But when the new wore off, when He began saying big grown-up things that were brave and blunt and threatening to their smug self-righteousness, they didn't like what they were hearing.

Jesus' ministry, though, was as broad as human need. It couldn't be confined to His family's expectations, His hometown, or His birth nation. And so already—here—at home—the desire to kill Him began.

ELIJAH AND ELISHA.
The story of Elijah and the widow is from 1 Kings 17:7-24. The story of Elisha and Naaman is found in 2 Kings 5:1-27.

KINGDOM OF GOD.
This is God taking His rightful place with human beings—one person at a time. At the end of time all other kingdoms will be defeated and destroyed.

4:31-44 The Power of His Word

Luke recorded four incidents in this section that took place in Capernaum, a kind of home base for Jesus' ministry in Galilee. Here Jesus showed His power over demons and physical diseases.

Verse 35. Why did Jesus tell the demon to be quiet? This evil spirit was actually saying things that were true—things some of the people in town needed to hear—like the fact that Jesus was "the Holy One of God." But in silencing the evil spirit, Jesus proved Himself to be its authority.

Luke 5

5:1-11 An Awesome Catch

For the first time in Luke's Gospel, we meet our old pal Simon, later called Peter. Yet, judging from the fact that Jesus had borrowed Simon's boat (verse 3), we assume that these two had already become somewhat acquainted.

Still, Jesus' command in verse 4 took Peter by surprise. You can imagine it. This is one of those cases where you've been working at something for a long time, then someone who (you think) knows a lot less about this than you do shows up, trying to tell you how to do everything right. But when you take his advice—and it works—then, well . . .

So the miraculous haul of fish struck Peter not only with awe at Jesus' power but with dismay at his own sinful condition. Peter's fearful retreat from Him was quite a contrast to the way many people try to nuzzle up so cozily and comfortably to Jesus today—sins and all. But in Peter's genuine shame and emptiness we see what a proper response to Christ's presence is supposed to look and feel like.

Jesus' reaction was equally stunning. Instead of dismissing Simon as a hopeless mess of mood swings, He almost playfully invited him to come be part of what He was doing—an even bigger fishing expedition, where the fishing nets even work on land . . . with people. What was Simon's (and James's and John's) answer to this? They left everything. We don't exactly know what leaving "everything" meant in their lives, but whatever it cost them, they meant for it to be a total commitment to Jesus.

From this passage, then, we see the basic steps in following Christ: *obedience* (verse 4), *confession* (verse 8), and *commitment* (verse 11).

When was the last time you were reading the Bible or hearing a sermon, and you felt God was expecting something of you that seemed too hard, nearly impossible? What was your response to Him?

_____

_____

_____

_____

5:12-16 Jesus Heals a Leper

Chances are, you've probably never seen a leper in the flesh (or what's left of his flesh). But maybe you've felt like one—alone, unloved, unwanted. No group in ancient society was more pitiful than the lepers. Their disease was a slow, lingering death. They died inch by inch. To make matters worse, lepers were cut off from the rest of society, including their families. Yet Jesus dared to touch this leper and to speak the word that caused him to be cured.

Jesus' order for the man to go and show himself to the priest was a way to validate the miracle. It was like getting a written letter from a doctor that declares the patient to be officially disease-free.

LEPROSY.
This included a variety of gross skin disorders, with symptoms ranging from white patches on the skin, to running sores, to the loss of whole fingers, toes, noses, ears, and other body parts.

CLEANSING RITUALS.
To read more about the interesting procedure Jesus was telling the leper to perform, go to Leviticus 14:1-32.

PHARISEES.
This was the largest and most influential of the three major Jewish parties, controlling the synagogues and holding people to the strictest letter of the law—or at least to their interpretation of it. The term literally means "separated ones," based on their practice of pulling away from other people to study and debate. Watch for them often. They viewed Jesus with suspicion from start to finish.

SCRIBES.
These "teachers of the law"—mostly Pharisees—were experts on Jewish history and tradition. They eventually took the lead in the plan to kill Jesus.

HUMAN DEPRAVITY.
When Jesus said He wasn't called to the "righteous," He didn't mean that there were some who were already good enough on their own not to need Him. The truth is that there are none who are righteous (Romans 3:10)—only those who think they are. All are in need of Christ's forgiveness (Romans 3:23).

5:17-26 Through the Roof

Jesus stunned the gathered snoops and dignitaries, not only by healing the paralyzed man, but also by claiming to forgive his sins. Because this is something only God can do, the scribes and Pharisees accused Jesus of blasphemy—of showing outright, unashamed disrespect for the character of God—in this case, by claiming to possess God's power Himself. In contrast to the religious leaders, though, the rest of the crowd was amazed at Jesus' miracle of healing and gave praise to God.

By connecting the man's sin with his sickness, Jesus was not saying that this guy's condition was a direct result of something bad he had done. Yet Jesus was meeting a need deeper than the man's desire to walk. His healed limbs were living pictures of what Christ had done on the inside . . . in the man's forgiven heart.

Plus, of course, this story is a great example of human friendship, of people who were so concerned for one guy's condition that they went all out to get him some help. A lot of people you know today are in *spiritual paralysis*. They need Jesus really bad. Are you willing to go "through the roof" to take them to Him?

5:27-32 Hanging Out with Sinners

Luke presents Jesus as the friend of sinners who freely associated with all kinds of people—placing Jesus on a collision course with the Pharisees, who considered such people unclean, unworthy of anything but scorn. So if you weren't popular, if you had a bad reputation, you could forget about getting any help from these guys. According to them, God wasn't interested in you until you got your act cleaned up a little.

In response to His critics, though, Jesus compared Himself to a doctor whose mission is directed toward the sick and needy, not the independently healthy. True Christianity has always shown itself best by the way it treats the least and the lowest.

Think of someone on your campus or in your town—or just someone in general who you would consider to be on the lowest social rung. How do you think Jesus would treat them? How do you treat them?

_____

_____

_____

5:33-39 A New Way of Thinking

Fast or Feast? (verses 33-35)

The Pharisees were in the habit of fasting—going without food—for two days a week (or at least going through the motions, using it as a convenient excuse for their crabby behavior). Such self-sacrifice wasn't easy on the stomach, but it apparently pumped their soul so full of pride that it made skipping a few meals well worth the hunger pangs. Jesus' explanation for why His disciples weren't big on this practice makes it clear that there are times for fasting and times for feasting, but never a good time for putting on a show.

Old vs. New (verses 36-39)

Jesus had come with a revolutionary new message—not one that could be patched onto an average life of law-keeping or maintained within normal expectations. He had come to embody a new covenant, to announce a coming kingdom that made sense of what God had been doing throughout the Old Testament. Living in this kingdom was not based on rules and restrictions but on faith and belief in Jesus. He was calling people to become totally new creations (2 Corinthians 5:17), not just reworked hand-me-downs with no way to stretch or make room for something bigger than what they'd always known.

FASTING.
The spiritual discipline of going without food for a period of time was most often done as a means of developing humility and dependence on God (Ezra 8:21-23) or seeking an answer to prayer (Acts 13:2-3). Jesus encouraged us to continue this practice as an act of private, refreshing devotion (Matthew 6:16-18).

WINESKINS.
These were dehaired skins of small animals (like goats), sewn together to hold wine or milk. Over time the skins lost some of their pliability, causing them to rip and burst as wine began to ferment inside of them.

6:1-11 Let Freedom Sting

Lord of the Sabbath (verses 1-5)

Keeping the Sabbath was near the top on the Pharisees' list of pious virtues—partly because it could be so easily measured and cracked down on. Sabbath-keeping in their book, you see, wasn't just a single rule but a whole bunch of banned activities—such as not being allowed to tie or untie a knot . . . stuff like that. But Jesus declared Himself "Lord of the Sabbath"—the One who made it, who thought it up in the first place. I mean, how'd you like to be the one who invented something, only to have somebody else come along to tell you that you don't know what you're doing with it? Crazy.

Verse 2. Is this the same Jesus who said He hadn't come to destroy the law? (Matthew 5:17-19). Then why does He seem to take such delight in flaunting His freedom over it? Are we as free to break the law as He seems to be? Or was Jesus perhaps not breaking anything but man-made traditions? Jesus would later say that the law could be boiled down to two things: loving God and loving others (Mark 12:29-31). He seems to be saying here that every day is a good day to feed the hungry and tend to the hurting.

Good Saturday (verses 6-11)

Jesus understood that the original intent of the Sabbath was to provide a day of rest for God's people. And who deserved rest more than those who were sick and suffering—no matter what day it was? And who could say it was a violation of the Sabbath to "do good" and to "save life"? Well, the Pharisees could, because their law-abiding worked against the very heart of God. It was Jesus' radical thinking on this that was stirring the fury of His critics, who were quickly becoming not just a bit annoyed but a bitter enemy.

SACRED BREAD.
This "bread of the Presence" was one of the items God had commanded to be kept continually in the temple—twelve loaves of them—perhaps representing the people of Israel standing before Him. It was replaced hot once a week, with the old bread reserved only for the priests to eat (Leviticus 24:5-9).

DAVID'S ARMY.
Jesus' story about David and his hungry fighting men comes from 1 Samuel 21:1-6.

6:12-16 Choosing of the Twelve

If you showed up at a job interview with the same lack of experience, potential, and references Jesus' disciples had, you'd find yourself back on the street in a hurry. But fortunately for them and for the rest of Christian history, Jesus didn't choose His friends based on their looks, their training, or their trumped-up resumé. He chose His companions after a whole night spent in prayer, with the full awareness that the Father had chosen these particular twelve for His own good reasons. What giants they all (but one) would turn out to be! And that one had been deliberately chosen for a whole other reason.

APOSTLES.
These are messengers sent out under another's authority. The word was most often used later, in speaking of those the risen Christ had sent out as witnesses of His resurrection. They were a subset of the larger group of disciples, which carries more of the idea of a "student."

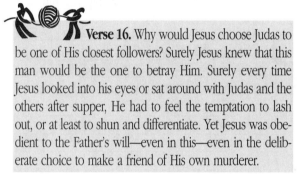

Verse 16. Why would Jesus choose Judas to be one of His closest followers? Surely Jesus knew that this man would be the one to betray Him. Surely every time Jesus looked into his eyes or sat around with Judas and the others after supper, He had to feel the temptation to lash out, or at least to shun and differentiate. Yet Jesus was obedient to the Father's will—even in this—even in the deliberate choice to make a friend of His own murderer.

6:17-49 The Sermon on the Plain

You'll recognize a lot of passages in this section as being identical to those from the Sermon on the Mount (Matthew 5–7). More than likely, though, this particular text was not from that same event (since this sermon is said to be delivered "on a level place," not a mountain). Perhaps it just covers teaching themes that Jesus returned to more than once with His disciples.

Blessings and Curses (verses 20-26)

The short statements in verses 20-23 are commonly called beatitudes—a word that just means "happy" or "blessed." Verses 24-26, on the other hand, are woes—the cursed consequences of living in conflict with God's values. (You'll see a ton more of these in Luke 11:39-52.) What you're seeing here is a common theme in Luke's Gospel—and in Jesus' teaching—where the values of God's kingdom are totally upside-down from our natural way of thinking. Let's look at some of them:

Not What You'd Expect

Expect Blessing From:	*Expect Trouble From:*
Being poor (6:20)	Being rich (6:24)
Being hungry (6:21)	Being full (6:25)
Weeping (6:21)	Laughter (6:25)
Being excluded, insulted (6:22)	Being spoken well of (6:26)
Loving your enemies (6:35)	Loving only friends (6:32)

What do unbelievers say about your church and about the Christians on your campus? Does anything Jesus says in this passage change the way you feel about being criticized or belittled because of your faith?

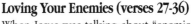

Loving Your Enemies (verses 27-36)

When Jesus was talking about "enemies" to the people in this culture, He didn't mean just next-door neighbors who sort of bugged you. He was talking about Roman troops who occupied their land, who took what they wanted without asking questions.

The closest we could probably get to it now on a personal level would be to think of them as bullies. Yet the love that's at the heart of Jesus' teaching is more than a command to have nice feelings toward our enemies (though that's part of it). It requires us to take deliberate action—to give more than is demanded, to do good things without expecting thanks, to model Jesus mercy—who loved us, remember, "while we were enemies" of His (Romans 5:10).

GOLDEN RULE.
The words "golden rule" don't appear in the Bible. But this principle, "do the same" for others [found in verse 31, as well as Matthew 7:12], was original and unique with Jesus, although forms of it appear [stated differently, in negative fashion] in the teachings of other religions.

Calling All Hypocrites (verses 37-49)

When Jesus told His followers not to "judge," He didn't mean that we can't make any value claims about what is right and wrong. In fact, we just have to look a few paragraphs down (to verses 43-44) to see that we can get a peek into people's hearts by observing the kind of "fruit" they bear—whether it's "good fruit" or "bad fruit."

But the big issue here is not about others' hearts; it's about ours. It's about being authentic, being who we say we are, avoiding hypocrisy and inconsistency at all costs. These are not threats to hold over someone else's head but warnings to keep in front of ourselves, so that we never judge in others what we let slip by in our own lives.

And if you ever fear that living a hypocrisy-free life is impossible, spend some time in verses 46-49. There's a rock-solid foundation available to those who are willing to dig deeply into the Word and build a life that's as strong on the inside as it appears on the outside.

JUDGING OTHERS.
Verse 37 is the new, favorite Bible quote of unbelievers in our culture: "Do not judge, and you will not be judged." So when you try to take a stand for Christ, don't be surprised to have this one thrown back in your face. It's true, of course: we're commanded not to be hypocrites. But it certainly doesn't mean that truth can't be defined and defended.

Luke 7

7:1-10 An Unexpected Faith

Maybe you know of a major influencer on your campus who (you suspect) is a Christian. He has so much going for him, though, that he's not the kind of guy who seems to need Jesus all that much. But one day he does something, or he says something, and suddenly everyone knows: this person is a true believer.

Much of this chapter shows how Jesus' found deep faith in some of the most unlikely people, yet found doubt growing in those from whom more was expected.

Start with the centurion. Here was a guy who under-

CENTURION.
He was a Roman officer, usually a career soldier, who commanded about 100 men ["cent-" is a prefix meaning 100]. Interestingly, all the centurions mentioned in the New Testament [Mark 15:39, Acts 10:1-48 and 27:3] seem to be pretty good guys.

stood the nature of Christ's authority, who saw no difference between a soldier following orders and a disease obeying its healer. Imagine what the crowd—and even Jesus' own disciples—thought when Jesus turned to them and basically said, "This Roman knows more about who I am than any of you do."

Capernaum
GALILEE
Sea of Galilee
Nazareth
Nain

MEDITERRANEAN SEA

Jordan River

a village in southwest Galilee

7:11-17 Putting the Fun in Funerals

You've been to funerals. You know how sad they are, how solemn and quiet, how hard it is to know what to say. That's probably what this widow thought until the day Jesus showed up at her only son's funeral.

Perhaps the most important thing to spot in this story—outside of Jesus' awesome power to restore life to a dead man (don't just gloss over that)—is His motivation for performing this miracle. All of His miracles were designed to glorify God, of course, but notice what else made Him want to help this woman: "He had compassion on her." Those who think of God as impersonal and unemotional should take a good look at Jesus—and see that this God of ours enjoys giving us good reason to put our tissues away.

RAISING THE DEAD.
The Gospels tell of two other people Jesus brought back from the dead: Jairus' daughter (Luke 8:40-56) and Lazarus (John 11:1-44). Only Christ, though, would be raised from the dead never to die again (Romans 6:9).

7:18-30 John's Questions, Jesus' Answers

The Question (verses 18-20)

The last time we saw John the Baptist was in 3:20, locked up in prison for calling Herod an adulterer (among other things). The isolation must have played tricks on John's confidence, though, because he found himself wondering if his whole reason for living had been a mistake, if he had been fooled into wasting his life on a lie. Isn't it interesting that someone as tough-talking as John the Baptist could get scared, could have doubts, could question whether he'd heard things right from God?

B.C. A.D.

HISTORY.
John in prison. In an account that closely parallels the New Testament, the Jewish historian Josephus confirmed that Herod arrested John and had him executed because "he feared that John's extensive influence over people might lead to an uprising."

The Answer (verses 21-23)

We often pray to God or read our Bibles knowing what we want to hear. Jesus responds to John (as He often does to us) by saying what he needed to hear.

Thinking back to some of John's earlier statements (3:7-9), perhaps he had expected Jesus to do a little more head-busting, to not be quite so busy healing and helping when He could be bringing lawbreakers to justice. But Jesus' reply to John—as it was so often to so many others—was bigger than the question. Many times in Scripture, Jesus didn't give a straight answer; He gave a better one. And those who may have been "offended" by it (verse 23) were expected to deal with the difference between what they wanted to hear and the truth he was telling them.

MESSIAH'S MINISTRY.
Verse 22 reveals that Jesus was fulfilling prophecy about what the Messiah would be like— sent to bring good news to the blind, the lame, the sick, the deaf, the dead, the poor. One really clear Old Testament link to this is found in Isaiah 29:18-19.

Something about Jesus didn't look the way John had expected. Do you ever feel that way? How do you square it when you read something Jesus said or did and . . . it just doesn't sound like Him?

_____

_____

_____

_____

The Upshot (verses 24-30)

In praising John the Baptist, though, Jesus again demonstrated the new, totally different way of thinking He came to proclaim. He told of the unexpected rewards that come from going against the flow of human nature—stuff like "the least in the kingdom" being the greatest in God's sight. The Pharisees weren't getting it—even John himself might have been a little confused by it—but the riffraff couldn't get enough.

JOHN'S BAPTISM.
Though it may have looked sort of the same, this baptism had a different purpose than the one we think of today. John's baptism was a practice initiated by God before Christ's death and resurrection to prepare people's hearts—through repentance — to receive Jesus as Savior.

7:31-35 Too Hard! No, Too Soft!

The next time you're gossiped about—by people in the church, no less—remember that Jesus knows exactly what it feels like. The Pharisees were talking behind His back all the time. That's because they were one-dimensional, black-and-white thinkers. It had to be their way or the highway. When they said, "Dance!" you danced. When they said, "Cry!" you cried. They knew (or at least they thought they knew) what true godliness was supposed to look like. And this Jesus just wasn't matching their picture of it (too happy). John the Baptist wasn't either (too radical). There was simply no pleasing these people who couldn't think any bigger than their own bias. But some in the crowd were able to see (verse 35) that Jesus was the living picture of truth.

JESUS' DEITY.
Again, as in 5:20-24, Jesus was declaring Himself to be God by exercising His authority to forgive sins. He didn't say, "God forgives you," but simply announced that the woman's "sins are forgiven" (verse 48). He was claiming deity for Himself.

7:36-50 A Woman's Worship

It wasn't uncommon for people in the street to come peek in on first-century parties. But to barge right in, to walk right up to one of the honored guests and make a spectacle of yourself in full view of everyone—this shocked the sensibilities of a religious man like Simon. Running Jesus through his Pharisee filter, then, Simon concluded that Jesus could no way be the Messiah. He should know who this sinful woman was. And He should never let someone like *that* do . . . *this!* . . . to *Him*.

But Jesus showed His true prophetic insight by reading the thoughts of Simon himself—and telling him a story that cut to the heart of his questions. The truth is, we have all been forgiven much. And those of us who are believers, but who may have a hard time being deeply in love with Jesus, have apparently forgotten that even good kids who come to Christ are born evil to the core—and need God's grace just as badly as those who've been headline sinners.

Simon knew the worst kind of life there is—going halfway with Jesus, feeling like he's a big man just because he was a little more open to Christ than his fellow Pharisees were, yet who stopped short before letting himself go all the way in worship. Maybe you've experienced that miserable feeling too. How freeing it is, though, to be like this woman—not to care what anyone thinks as long as Jesus is pleased and God is glorified.

MARY OF BETHANY?
Some people have identified this woman either as Mary Magdalene or Mary of Bethany, Martha and Lazarus's sister. However, there is no compelling evidence to support these claims. Mary of Bethany later anointed Jesus (John 12:2-8), but the details of these two anointings are different.

Have you ever wished you had a powerful testimony like those who've been saved from truly eye-popping sins? Can a person who's received Christ at a young age ever love God the way these people do?

_____

_____

_____

_____

Luke 8

8:1-3 Ministry Update

WOMEN.
Jesus had come into a culture where women were mostly confined to the home and family, with little access to the rest of society. Yet Jesus treated them with dignity. Unlike the common man of His day, He recognized women as valuable and elevated their status as full participants in His kingdom.

Luke drops in a short summary of Jesus' ministry up to this point—including the interesting sidelight that others were "supporting [Jesus and His disciples] from their possessions" (verse 3).

The truth is, Jesus didn't need any help. Yet here's the Creator of the universe, who could have made bread out of rock piles if He wanted to, letting others share in the drama of His life, allowing Himself to be cooked for and cleaned up after by those He had created. He didn't need them, really. But they needed Him. He still blesses us today, in fact, by allowing us to serve Him.

PARABLES.
These are stories that capture spiritual truth in earthly examples. Jesus used three different types of these: [1] short sayings, like when He called believers "the salt of the earth," [2] simple parables, when He would describe, for example, why "the kingdom of heaven is like a mustard seed," and [3] narrative parables, fully played-out stories like this one, rich with spiritual insight.

8:4-15 Parable of the Sower

You can think of this parable not in terms of others' hearts but of your own. It's like when you go on a retreat and come face-to-face with who you really are, when God peels away all your pretenses and shows you the true condition of your heart. Jesus' teaching throughout Luke (perhaps most clearly seen in 6:37-42) was often intended to make people examine their own motives and desires. He knows how easy it is for us to spot sin in someone else while leaving our own untouched.

But there's another way to look at it, too. Maybe you've heard this story used as a model for what happens when you talk with other people about Jesus. You faithfully share the gospel, yet the good news lands in different kinds of hearts—some hard, some rocky, some thorn-infested, some rich and fertile. And for those with hearts ready to receive it, the word takes hold, bearing a hundred times over. So even though many will reject what you say, keep telling them about Jesus, because those with willing hearts will more than make up for the ones who took what you said and did nothing with it.

But either way you approach this parable, the same four kinds of ground apply. Everyone's heart is in one of these conditions. We need to know where ours is, as well:

- "The path"—a heart totally closed off to Christ
- "The rock"—someone who believes in God until it costs them something
- "The thorns"—with too much other stuff going on to keep focused on God
- "Good ground"—where the word is not only received but retained. Work to keep your heart like that.

Verse 10. You may say, "I thought Jesus told parables so people could more easily understand what He was trying to say. So how come He says that the reason He did it was to make people even more confused, so that 'looking they may not see, and hearing they may not understand'?" The answer to this question centers around the fact that Jesus knew people's hearts. He knew the ones who wouldn't accept the truth, even if it was right in front of their faces. In every generation there are people who won't believe no matter what you say.

Verse 12. Jesus said the Devil "takes away the word" from people's hearts. Does the Devil really have the power to do that? I mean, can a person have Jesus one day and lose Him the next? Or five years later? Or anytime in life? No. Jesus said the Devil does this to people "so that they may not believe and be saved." Therefore, Jesus was referring to people who don't truly believe yet, people who may like a little of what they hear about Jesus but not enough to jump in with both feet—the only way you can come into a relationship with Christ.

8:16-18 Carry the Light

Be careful not to disconnect this passage from the parable Jesus just told. He is still talking about the heart—especially the secrets of the heart, our true character and motives. He's talking about the importance of listening to the word of God—which means more than just *hearing* it but also *obeying* it—and about the incredible amount of spiritual growth that can occur in our lives when we take His word seriously.

Those who hear Him and receive this word deep within their hearts now have a light inside—a light that should never be covered up or embarrassed about, but revealed—so that others will be drawn to it out of the darkness.

LOONY?
In another account of this story (Mark 3:20-21), Jesus' family said they came looking for Him because they thought He'd gone crazy. That's not surprising, since some of them didn't believe their brother was who He claimed to be anyway (John 7:5). Jesus learned to live with being misunderstood.

8:19-21 Extended Family

Continuing with this theme of *listening* for what God is saying, Jesus declared that His family was not made up of people who were born into a certain class or bloodline, but those "who hear and do the word of God." It's a distinction that can cause clashes even between people who live under the same roof, like when Christian parents must struggle to hold their rebellious child to biblical standards, or when a believing wife must maintain her commitment to Christ against her husband's wishes.

> How do you show respect to people in your own family—maybe an uncle or cousin, maybe even a brother, sister, or parent—who don't approve of your Christianity? What do you do with that conflict?

_____

_____

_____

8:22-25 Storm at Sea

Now for a string of several miracles that show Jesus' power over downdrafts, demons, disease, and even death itself.

As far as this first story goes, if you've ever been out on a boat during a thunderstorm, you know how the disciples felt—terrified! And if you've read about Jesus' ability to work miracles, you're not surprised at how *He* reacted to the high wind—by sleeping through it. But nobody is quite prepared for the disciples' question after Jesus got up and told the waves to pipe down. "Who can this be?" they asked themselves. *What?!* They had already been with Him for months—had seen Him heal the sick and raise the dead—had heard Him preach with God-breathing authority. Yet strangely, even these men who were closest to Him still didn't really understand who Jesus was and what He was about.

8:26-39 Demons at Bay

This next miracle is the second time in Luke that Jesus has faced down a demon. (It won't be the last.) Jesus is always victorious over them, because even in all their scary shooting-off at the mouth, they have no power to resist the word of God, spoken in authority by Jesus Himself.

The sad part of this story is the reaction of the townspeople to the man's deliverance. Instead of falling down in worship, in awe and gratitude for rescuing their village from this raving lunatic, they were so bound by superstition and dread that they begged Jesus to leave. "Gripped by great fear," they pushed away the one who had the power to deliver *them* from bondage as well.

The *healed* man was no longer afraid, however, and wanted to go with Him. Still, Jesus knew that this man actually needed to stay—where those who had seen him up close, or had heard him howling in the distance, could have a constant reminder of the day Jesus came . . . and changed everything.

8:40-48 Healed by a Touch

Notice how incredibly sensitive Jesus is to human need. First came the request from a distraught father, begging Him to come heal his daughter, who was "at death's door." But even while heading off with this man—focused on this one critical situation—He still remained aware of another who needed His touch. He took time to stop. He took time to listen. He took time for anyone who needed Him . . . anytime.

8:49-56 Touched by a Healer

Then suddenly, along the road, arrived the worst news a father could hear: His daughter was dead. He had missed his last moments with her, out trying to get help. The healer had failed him, let him down, chosen a grown woman

DEMONS.
Most of the biblical references to this kind of demonic control appear in the Gospels, probably because of an outburst of satanic opposition to Jesus. Demon possession showed itself in various ways, but the cure was always in the power of Christ, not in magic rites. Especially in foreign countries, missionaries continue to see some of this activity today— and still claim victory in Jesus' name.

LEGION.
This was a Roman military term that described the elite soldiers in the army, usually numbering about 4,500 to 6,000 men out of the entire force. Were there that many demons in this guy? Maybe.

for healing and let a little twelve-year-old girl—with her whole life ahead of her—slip away without doing all He could.

Perhaps for a moment, the man felt angry at Jesus. *If He had just hurried and kept up with me! If He just hadn't let Himself get sidetracked!* The report of the girl's death wasn't entirely unexpected, but still—*He could have done something!*

"But when Jesus heard it, He answered him, 'Don't be afraid. Only believe, and she will be made well.' " Some of us are overly afraid of death, so we are held hostage to it. Jesus is totally confident in life, so He lives in constant victory. And therefore we who believe in Him have nothing to fear. We must "only believe."

Verse 56. Why would Jesus go to all the trouble of healing this girl, then make her parents promise "to tell no one what had happened"? Boy, that's a really good question, and no one can say for sure why. But here are a few maybes. Maybe He knew that "healing stories" are like "fish stories"—they tend to get bigger and more exaggerated every time they're told. Maybe He wanted the little girl to bear the eyewitness report herself. Maybe He knew that seeing a resurrected kid with your own eyes paints a thousand words. Maybe?

Does dying scare you? Maybe. Or maybe not yet. But what do you think the people who have died believing in Christ would say to those who fear it so? Do you think death might be like other fears—not as bad as we thought it would be?

Luke 9

9:1-6 The Big Mission Trip

Ever been on a mission trip? That's what this excursion is. And just like your message when you go to another state or country, the message the twelve disciples took "from village to village" had the full power of Jesus behind it. It was more than words, really. It was the kingdom of God in action. Their words carried the weight of Jesus' kingly authority, and those who rejected His royal proclamation did so at their own peril.

9:7-9 Jesus Who?

This is not the same Herod who tried to trick the wise men into leading him to baby Jesus (Matthew 2:1-7), but it is the same one John the Baptist rebuked for being an adulterer (3:19) and who will show up later in Jesus' life, gleefully demeaning Him in public at one of the court trials before His crucifixion (23:7-12). Throughout his entire reign Herod perceived Jesus as a constant threat to his power and looked for ways to kill Him. But Jesus was too sly for "that fox" (13:32).

9:10-17 The Feeding of the Five Thousand

Imagine it's late afternoon. You got up too late to have breakfast this morning. You had to study through lunch. You had a practice of some sort after school, and now it's "late in the day" and you've had nothing to eat. That's how hungry the people in this story were.

ELIJAH.
He was one of the most well-known of the Old Testament prophets; his story covers several chapters from 1 Kings 17 through 2 Kings 2. He and John the Baptist were a lot alike—hard-nosed, thick-skinned—and were tied together by an interesting prophecy from Malachi 4:5-6.

JOHN'S DEATH.
Read Mark 6:14-29 to get the full account of what happened in John's final hours.

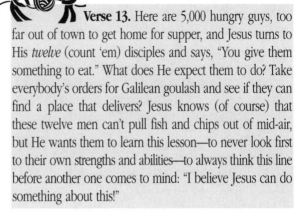

Verse 13. Here are 5,000 hungry guys, too far out of town to get home for supper, and Jesus turns to His *twelve* (count 'em) disciples and says, "You give them something to eat." What does He expect them to do? Take everybody's orders for Galilean goulash and see if they can find a place that delivers? Jesus knows (of course) that these twelve men can't pull fish and chips out of mid-air, but He wants them to learn this lesson—to never look first to their own strengths and abilities—to always think this line before another one comes to mind: "I believe Jesus can do something about this!"

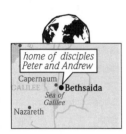

home of disciples
Peter and Andrew
Capernaum
GALILEE ● Bethsaida
Sea of
Galilee
Nazareth

D-

CREATIONISM.

The fact that Jesus could create bread that was already baked and fish that were already grown proves that He can create something that already has an age—like Adam, for example, who was created as a man, right? Not a fetus. Unlike evolutionary theories, which say life began as tiny particles that developed over time into more complex forms, our Creator could have created the whole earth to have a built-in age from the very beginning. Perhaps the world is not billions and billions of years old—it just looks like it.

This is the only miracle reported in all four of the Gospels, and it marks a turning point in Jesus' ministry. Up to this time, Jesus had been circulating fairly freely among the various towns and villages, annoying the religious officials but astounding the masses with miracles and healings and incredible displays of power. Very soon, however, the crowds would start dwindling. His popularity numbers would drop. The way was about to get very tough, and you'll see Him devoting more and more of His time to teaching His disciples, preparing their hearts for what's coming, getting ready for the reason He came here.

9:18-20 The Light Comes On

Notice how prayer is just a natural part of life for Jesus— how He moves from talking to God to talking to His friends in one fluid motion. But focus also on His two questions. The first one is more general and gets a Sunday school answer. The second one is more personal, and the room goes quiet—except for one who was brave enough to speak his heart. Certainly Peter still might be thinking that Jesus was the Messiah of popular Jewish expectations, who had come to run the Romans out of Israel. But, he was getting closer to the truth. He was getting real with Jesus.

Who do you say Jesus is?
Put Him in your own words.

_____

_____

_____

_____

9:21-27 This Is Gonna Cost You

Is there someone you admire as a really strong Christian, and when you're with this person, all you have is respect for him? But if he started coming around you and your friends more, you'd feel sort of embarrassed that you know him? I mean, there's a place for being that serious about your faith and all, but sometimes—when you and your friends are just wanting to cut up and have fun—you wouldn't really want that person around.

Jesus knew this was the way we'd be tempted to feel about Him sometimes. But, hey, this is part of the high calling of faith. It may cost us being popular. It may cost us doing some of the things our friends expect of us. Better *that*, though, than having Christ be ashamed of *us*—the way we are sometimes ashamed of Him.

This is a critical passage in Luke. For the first time, Jesus began letting His closest followers in on the reality of what was to come—not just for Him but for all those who claimed Him as Lord—us included. Like before, He talked in upside-down terms—denying yourself, embracing your burden, losing your life—yet He promised that these things offered more than "the whole world" has to offer. The Christian faith cost Jesus His life. What will it cost us?

SON OF MAN.
This was one of Jesus' favorite descriptions of Himself, emphasizing His full humanity and His mission as the substitute sacrifice for people's sin. He was Son of God, yet also Son of Man.

TRANSFIGURED.
We use the more common term "transformed" in everyday English. It comes from the same Greek word from which we get "metamorphosis."

TABERNACLE.
Think of it as church on wheels. This movable tent structure was the portable worship center for the Israelites throughout their many years of wandering from place to place. The cloud of God's presence descended on it when they were stationary, then lifted to lead them to their next destination (Exodus 40:34-38).

9:28-36 The Transfiguration

Prayer (just like in verse 18) again preceded a key moment in Jesus' life. This dazzling display of His glory and brilliance—this blinding picture of His purity and power—must have blown away the three close disciples He had brought to the mountain, proving again that Jesus was God in flesh.

Yet imagine how encouraging this event was to Jesus Himself. After months of being constantly surrounded by those who either hated Him or (at best) barely understood His mission, these two great Bible heroes must have been like old friends coming for a visit. Their familiar faces and reassuring words renewed His confidence, inspiring Him to complete His calling. As God, He had created these men and directed their lives. As man, He humbly received their friendship and let them minister to His spirit.

Throughout Bible history "the cloud" (verse 34) was a picture of God's presence and a place where His secrets were both concealed and revealed. Everyone on the mountain of transfiguration (quite possibly Mount Hermon, a towering peak at the northern rim of Israel's border) heard the Father's voice speaking from the thick mist. Imagine the electricity that still raced in their hearts when the cloud lifted, when the darkness resettled, when Jesus was left standing alone there beside them.

9:37-42 Another Demon Bites the Dust

Why couldn't the disciples do this themselves? We know from verse 1 of this chapter that Jesus had given them "power and authority over all demons, and to heal diseases." So . . . what's the problem here? Whether it was fear, whether it was weakness, whether it was pride that had been building up over the past few weeks of success—whatever it was—Jesus seemed to include His own followers (as well as everyone else within earshot) in His harsh rebuke. Jesus loves us, and He forgives us, but Jesus is serious about our doing what He's called and equipped us to do.

9:43-45 A Painful Prophecy

With His betrayer perhaps hanging on every word, Jesus gave His little cluster of twelve disciples a chance to "let these words sink in." You wonder if Judas was in the process of sinking Him already.

9:46-50 Haves and Have Nots

Nothing ever surprises Jesus. But surely this saddened Him—His disciples reacting to His prediction of personal suffering by drawing up petty turf battles over who's in the club and who's number one. Jesus' response back to them? "Don't want Me just *for* yourself, and don't want Me *all* to yourself." It doesn't take much, really, to be great in God's eyes.

This doesn't mean that we shouldn't ever strive to be leaders. *We should!* But we should never want to be great at the cost of making others feel unimportant. True leaders are able to help everyone be the best they can be.

PROGRESSIVE REVELATION. God usually makes Himself known to people gradually. Throughout the Old Testament, He revealed Himself little by little ... until Jesus came and provided a full expression of what God is like (Hebrews 1:1-3). In the same way, He conceals some things from us until we are able to understand them (verse 45). This is not God's way of holding out on us. It's His way of not forcing us to carry burdens we're not ready to bear.

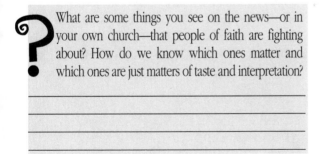

What are some things you see on the news—or in your own church—that people of faith are fighting about? How do we know which ones matter and which ones are just matters of taste and interpretation?

_____

_____

_____

_____

SAMARITANS.
Officially these were citizens of Samaria, a mountainous region about forty miles north of Jerusalem. But the bad blood was so great between them and the Jews—because of their pagan worship and their intermarriage with other nations—that Jewish people traveling between Galilee and Judea would take the long way around to avoid setting foot in Samaritan territory.

9:51-56 A Journey to Jerusalem

Jesus had given the name "sons of thunder" to brothers James and John (Mark 3:17), apparently because of their blustery, explosive temperaments. You certainly see it coming out here—in their angry reaction to the Samaritans' cold shoulder. From this we gather the unusual notion that hotheads are certainly welcome in Christ's service, but they may have a harder time than others. It may be tough for them to hold their tempers in check and leave judgment in the hands of God. So Jesus is not opposed to someone having a little fire in the belly, but it can never be fueled by arrogance or ambition.

9:57-62 Wanting It All, Wanting It Now

Seeing bands of followers trailing around after a wandering rabbi wasn't all that uncommon in Jesus' day. Still, His demands were serious and severe—then as now. They call for giving up everything—safety, security, the option of sinning even in small doses. And they call for doing it now, not after you've had a chance to tank up on life for a while. This is not about riding the coattails of your parents' faith. This is between you and Jesus—for all the marbles. It's about putting your "hand to the plow" and never looking back.

Luke 10

10:1-16 The Even Bigger Mission Trip

Remember the big mission trip from the first part of chapter 9? Jesus now widened His ministry team, selecting several dozen others to spread His kingdom's message throughout the region of Galilee and beyond. Their commission was one of "peace" (verse 5), but to those who reject Christ's words, the judgment is terrifying: eternal death, eternal separation from God.

And it's not just for the big-time, hard-core sinners! You probably know a lot of people who are pretty good guys and girls, who live fairly moral lives even *without* Jesus in their hearts. But His hard words for the Jewish cities in Galilee—Chorazin, Bethsaida, Capernaum—showed that the dastardly deeds of Sodom (homosexuality and such—Genesis 19:4-5) and of Tyre and Sidon (home of wicked queen Jezebel—1 Kings 16:31) were not as heinous as this: the sin of an otherwise decent person rolling his eyes at the saving love of Christ.

10:17-24 Good Work, Guys

Field Reports (verses 17-20)
The teams returned home with great stories to tell, and Jesus was pleased. His reaction may not sound like it to you, though. But His words were not a criticism, not the sour grapes of someone who's never satisfied. They were more of an appeal to keep things in perspective. You see, watching demons fly back to the hell-hole they came from? That's pretty cool. But being saved from sin and promised a plate at an invitation-only dinner in the kingdom of heaven? Nothing can top that!

Sidon

Tyre

perhaps as old as 2000 B.C.

Capernaum

GALILEE

Sea of Galilee

MEDITERRANEAN S.

PHOENICIA

OMNISCIENCE.
We say a lot when we say God is omniscient (all-knowing), because He knows everything that is, and has been, and will be. He also knows everything that might have been, everything that could be. His predictions of what could happen to people who won't repent (verse 13) are not just guesses or projections. They are examples of His complete knowledge of every possibility.

SATAN'S FALL.
We don't know a lot about this mysterious occurrence, but the best picture we get of it (besides verse 18) comes from Isaiah 14:12-20, of a "morning star" being flung to the earth, apparently before the creation of man. This "ancient serpent" gets his ultimate freefall in Revelation 12:7-9.

A Royal Welcome (verses 21-24)

How neat to watch Jesus worshiping! Here He praised the Father for His wisdom and grace and celebrated the unity that exists between the two of them. God has given the Son the privilege of revealing truth to His people. How Jesus must love sharing such great things with His friends.

10:25-37 The Good Samaritan

This story deals with questions like: How uncool is it to stand up for someone who's unpopular? What's it like to be stuck without a ride home after school and someone you don't like very much offers you a lift? When you're hurting and in immediate need, do you discriminate against the person who shows up first to help?

And then there's this question: Who is my neighbor? That's really the main point of this familiar parable. It's a story of prejudice, of racial hatred, of dislike for another individual based on no other crime than his place of birth—and how even a bigotry this bad can be obliterated in a matter of moments. Meet the players:

- "An expert in the law"—hiding behind all the right answers for all the wrong reasons
- A traveling "man"—obviously a Jewish guy on a trip through bandit-infested territory
- "A priest"—one of the high-ranking overseers of the people's sacrifices
- "A Levite"—a temple assistant well-schooled in all things ceremonial and proper
- "A Samaritan"—the most unexpected source of compassion for a Jew down on his luck

Once the story was told, the legal scholar could do nothing but mumble another of his right answers, having been painted into a corner by Jesus' heavenly logic—which was now as airtight as the packed dirt on a desert highway. "Who is my neighbor?" Not just those of a certain skin color, or a certain style of clothes, or a certain economic class. Our obligation is to be kind to everyone.

QUESTIONS.
When people tried to trap Jesus with questions, one of His best ways of responding to them was to come back with a question. And still today, when people are not really wanting the truth but just trying to trip you up, a question lobbed back into their court is a good way to keep the ball rolling.

ROAD TO JERICHO.
The 17-mile road from Jerusalem to Jericho drops more than 1,000 feet. It was wild country, with plenty of places for robbers to hide.

DENARII.
One denarius was a small silver coin equal to a day's wage for a common laborer.

The Jews considered the Samaritans a bunch of lowlifes. What cast of characters might Jesus use if He were to tell this same story today and use people from your region of the country or your neighborhood?

_____

_____

_____

_____

10:38-42 Mary and Martha

As it's often said, there are two kinds of people. And in this case you're looking at one person who's focused on doing and another one who's content with just being. Martha wasn't just working; she was working herself up into a wad, probably slamming dishes to make sure everyone knew she was BUSY BACK HERE! But work that's done with the wrong attitude, with a victim mentality, is never pleasing to the Lord. A heart that stays open to what God is saying—no matter what you're doing—is a heart God can use.

Luke 11

11:1-13 Prayer Training

The Model Prayer (verses 1-4)

When Jesus prayed, you could feel it. It wasn't just words. It wasn't just something He did because He felt guilty if He didn't. It was the kind of praying that made someone listening nearby want to say, "Show me how you do that." Jesus' response to this request was not flowery and excessive. He simply stated some very basic things we can go to the Father with:

- Worship—recognition of His holy "name" and authority
- Confidence—resting in the hope of His coming "kingdom" and His kept promises

LORD'S PRAYER.
Luke's account of this prayer is a little shorter than the more common form found in Matthew 6:9-13. Either Jesus spoke these on separate occasions (the context is certainly different for both) or Luke chose to highlight certain aspects of it. The familiar refrain that begins "for thine is the kingdom" may have actually been added to later manuscripts of Matthew's Gospel.

- Personal needs—asking for the basic things required for "each day"
- Humility—confessing our sins, as well as asking for His strength in helping us forgive "everyone in debt to us"
- Dependence—trusting Him to protect us from the situations that cause us "temptation," even the kind we tend to bring on ourselves

The Model of Persistence (verses 5-8)

But a model prayer wasn't the only advice Jesus had for the one who said, "Teach us to pray." His parable of the two neighbors painted a living example of what happens when we realize how truly dependent we are on God, when we keep coming back and keep coming back—knowing we have no other source of provision, no plan B, no reason to doubt that God will give us "as much as [we need]."

Verse 7. Hard to picture praying to God and hearing Him bark back, "Don't bother me," isn't it? Is He really that reluctant to respond to a genuine problem of ours? Is that the image Jesus is portraying of the Father in this parable? No, He's merely saying (as He'll restate in verses 11-13) that if even the crusty neighbor next door knows when your *heart* is in your prayer, imagine how God—who knows every intent of your *heart*—responds when He sees real faith in one of His followers.

The Model Father (verses 9-13)

This is another section of Scripture that also appears as part of the three-chapter chunk in Matthew (5–7) known as the Sermon on the Mount. This one picks up on the "persistence" theme from the previous parable, instructing us not only to *ask* God for what we need but to "keep asking"; not to search for Him once or twice but to "keep searching"; not to knock a time or two but to "keep knocking." For on the other side of our prayers is a Father more eager to meet our needs than the best father on earth we can think of.

11:14-23 A House Divided

What Jesus proves in this passage is ultimate authority. Demons had the ability to do wickedly powerful things, like making this man "unable to speak." But with Jesus in his face, a demon was forced to tangle with "one stronger than he"—one who had no need to resort to cheap exorcism tricks but could send hell's angels packing with a word. When the jealous bystanders whispered that He was doing these deeds by witchcraft, Jesus ("knowing their thoughts") turned their weak-kneed arguments over on top of themselves, using the holes in their own faulty logic to slice their shallow defenses to shreds.

11:24-28 Empty Houses

The best thing that can happen to a person possessed by demons is not just to have the demons disappear. The best thing that can happen—to any of us—is to be filled with the Holy Spirit. People's hearts are empty vessels, waiting to be filled by something or someone. But when that "someone" is the Spirit of the living God, activated in us at salvation, we are no longer a welcome mat for Satan's lies and distortions. We are power plants, able to live in ongoing victory over the forces of darkness and evil.

BEELZEBUL.
This is the New Testament name for Satan—a variation of the Old Testament (Hebrew) word Baal-zebub, meaning "lord of the flies." In the language of the New Testament (Greek), this term may mean something like "lord of the dwelling" or more likely "lord of the dung" (Gross). Whatever, it's definitely not a compliment, and it's definitely a slam at Satan.

BLASPHEMY.
Keep verse 15 in mind when you get to 12:10, because Jesus makes it plain there (as if He doesn't make it plain enough here) that calling God's work evil is serious sin.

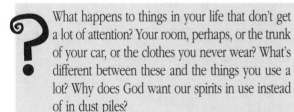

What happens to things in your life that don't get a lot of attention? Your room, perhaps, or the trunk of your car, or the clothes you never wear? What's different between these and the things you use a lot? Why does God want our spirits in use instead of in dust piles?

_____

_____

_____

JONAH.
His story (found in the Old Testament book that bears his name) is a historical event, yet it foreshadows the resurrection of Christ—three days in darkness, followed by a miraculous comeback.

QUEEN OF THE SOUTH.
Also called the "queen of Sheba," this wealthy dignitary brought her caravan hundreds of miles up the Arabian spice trade route to Jerusalem from the area now known as Yemen (1 Kings 10:1-13). Her trip was partly commercial, partly curiosity at the well-known wisdom of Israel's King Solomon.

RITUAL WASHING.
This little hand-washing routine before meals (verse 38) was not a biblical, Old Testament mandate but (as Mark 7:3 puts it) "the tradition of the elders." It was just one among many, "like the washing of cups, jugs, copper utensils, and dining couches" (Mark 7:5) that made up an impossible list of unnecessary rules.

11:29-32 The Sign of Jonah

In verse 16, some were demanding that Jesus give them some kind of "sign from heaven"—(as if feeding 5,000 people with a sack lunch or sending demons into a herd of pigs wasn't enough). That's because no sign is sufficient for those who refuse to believe—not a man spewed out of a whale's belly, not a king (Solomon) whose wisdom and teaching send cold chills down your back—not even a man dying on a cross one Friday afternoon and coming back to life the next Sunday morning.

There's no doubt that "something greater than Jonah is here!" Jonah, you recall, would have been just as happy if the people of Ninevah had paid him no attention and died in their unrepented sins. Jesus, though, was building up to the most grand display of love and power history would ever see. And He dearly wanted His hearers to receive the salvation He had come to win for them.

11:33-36 Daylight and Dark

This is a teaching about "light"—the power and purity of living in Christ. It's also about "darkness"—the destructive hopelessness that results from everything else. More than anything, though, it's about becoming a complete person whose "whole body" is filled with God's love and set free to be genuine. Jesus offers you a "whole body" experience—the satisfaction of being the same person at church as you are at school, of being totally His no matter where you are or what others may want you to be.

11:37-54 Woe!

Back in 6:24-26, Jesus gave His disciples some general warnings—"woes"—about the unhappy results of certain kinds of decisions and lifestyles. The woes in this passage, though, get a little more specific, targeted at certain sins

Jesus spotted in those who thought they had so little room for improvement:

- insincerity (verses 39-40)
- stinginess (41)
- legalism (42)
- arrogance (43)
- phoniness (44)
- double standards (46)
- self-righteousness (47-51)
- prejudice (52)

In a word, these religious professionals were fakes, showing one kind of face to the world while being totally opposite people inside. Yet instead of their hearts breaking over their own hypocrisy, they became defensive and insulted, "lying in wait" to catch Jesus in a slip-up.

ABEL AND ZECHARIAH.
Abel was the second son of Adam, killed by his jealous brother Cain for offering a sacrifice that pleased the Lord [Genesis 4:1-8]. Zechariah [not the Bible book Zechariah] was a prophet who confronted a king about his idolatry and paid for it with his life [2 Chronicles 24:20-22].

Luke 12

12:1-12 To Fear or Not to Fear

Hypocrites in Hiding (verses 1-3)

Perhaps you have a teacher with a blatant agenda, one who is simply out to shock you and discourage you in your faith. The Pharisees could be like that—stern, relentless, difficult, hard on their fellow Jews.

Or maybe you have a teacher who's a real hypocrite, who claims to be Christian but sure doesn't act like one. The Pharisees could be like that, too. Their words could sound so right, but their behavior told another story. Jesus warned His followers to beware the teachings of the Pharisees (Matthew 16:6-12), to watch what kind of tasteless lives were really produced by those who depended on empty rules and appearances.

Healthy Fear (verses 4-7)

"A crowd of many thousands" was still gathered around (verse 1), but Jesus continued talking to His own disciples

YEAST.
This small portion of fermented dough—known as "yeast" or "leaven"—is what makes bread rise. But because of its ability to change the nature of bread by introducing something old and rotten into it, yeast became linked in New Testament thought with evil influences and corruption—sins or teachings that poisoned and polluted.

HELL.

The Greek word for "hell" in verse 5 is gehenna—the "valley of Hinnom"—a ravine on Jerusalem's south side once used for pagan worship and (in Jesus' day) converted to a garbage dump.

AFTER DEATH.

Some don't believe in a literal hell but in what's called annihilationism—that at death we just sort of evaporate, cease to exist. But Jesus is clear that there is a place of eternal judgment for the unbelieving soul—"outer darkness" (Matthew 8:12), a "blazing furnace" (Matthew 13:42), where "there will be weeping and gnashing of teeth" (Luke 13:28).

HOLY SPIRIT.

He is the third member of the Trinity, comprised of Father, Son, and Holy Spirit. This whole book doesn't have enough room to describe Him, much less this little sidebar, but He is fully and eternally God—God in us—acting, revealing His will, and empowering us for service.

off to the side, preparing them to face crowds that before long would be turning hostile and threatening.

Peer pressure, you see, is nothing new. But when we give people permission to control our attitudes and behaviors, we are yielding control to someone unworthy of that kind of power—like the Pharisees, in this context. God alone, who knows everything about us and still loves us, is the only one worthy to control what we think, say, and do. He alone has ultimate power and control, even the "authority to throw [us] into hell." So we should have a healthy fear of Him, a sense of reverence, awe, and respect. And gratitude that He has chosen to love and protect us.

Feel the Spirit (verses 8-12)

Some of you may be ashamed to have your parents drop you off at a school function or to give you a hug and a kiss in public, to tell you they love you. C'mon. Are you ashamed of Jesus too? Don't disown Him—anywhere, for any reason—not after all He's done for you.

Something else to watch for in this passage is how Jesus begins to reveal the ministry of the Holy Spirit to His followers. The Spirit is the One who empowers Jesus to perform supernatural miracles and defeat the forces of Satan, as well as the One who makes the Word of God real to us, who helps us make sense of its mysteries, who enables us to do things we couldn't have done by ourselves.

Verse 10. You've probably heard this called the unpardonable sin—the one unholy act of men that "will not be forgiven." But what is the unpardonable sin? Could we be guilty of it and not realize it? There's a lot of debate on what the unpardonable sin means, but it boils down to this: attributing to Satan something God has obviously done. It's not a one-time occurrence but a lifetime pattern of unbelief and ridicule. Those who continually see good as evil, and evil as good, will die in their unbelief with no hope for their hardened, resistant souls. Christians, then, can be guilty of sin but not of this one.

12:13-21 Rich Man, Poor Man

Again, Jesus responded to one person's self-centered request with an answer that's even bigger than the question—a warning against "all greed" and the mistaken notion that money is the root of all happiness. To the rich man in this parable, money is something to "store"—a word that crops up four times in this passage. But money is *not* something to be stored. It is to be shared, to be invested in greater things, to be used for God's purposes. And those who have little of it can still be "rich toward God."

When you look down the road and imagine what your adult life will be like, how many of your expectations revolve around money and things? Which of your future dreams are the most pleasing to God?

_____

_____

_____

12:22-34 Why Worry?

Like greed, worry is a condition that's as real today as it was in Jesus' lifetime. His generation may have been worried about different things than we are—like where their next meal was coming from—but we have our own concerns to deal with. Jesus is saying that we can save ourselves a lot of trouble by letting God take care of the details.

Watch for two key statements in this passage: (1) "You of little faith"—it's a phrase Jesus used often, because faith is the main thing He's looking for in us. Everything else that's good in our lives flows out of our faith in God. The Christian life is not so much about being committed as it is about being submitted. (2) "Seek His kingdom"—again, He's not saying that Christianity is easy, but He is saying

SOLOMON.
He was the tenth son of David and succeeded his father as king of Israel (1 Kings 1—2). He is most remembered for his wisdom, his building of the temple, his incredible wealth, and his boatload of wives. He is also believed to have written Song of Songs (or Song of Solomon) and most of Proverbs.

that it's simple. When we focus on Him and trust His Word, everything else just sort of falls into place.

SLAVERY.
The Old Testament law permitted slavery but commanded that slaves were to be well-treated and given opportunities to earn their freedom, if desired—which was more than what other cultures did. Slavery was accepted throughout the ancient world and became a metaphor for unquestioning obedience to Christ.

D-🏠

SECOND COMING.
Some people think it's nonsense that Jesus is ever coming back to avenge sin. This position is also exposed in 2 Peter 3:1-13, using Noah's generation as an example of those who scoffed at his warning yet paid a deep-water price. God's delay, though, is actually a sign of His mercy and patience, not His weakness. He will "come like a thief" and redeem His people.

12:35-48 High Alert

We know about being "heads-up" from our brushes with terrorist threats, yet our culture still approaches most of life with a cool "whatever-ness." We shouldn't. Too many of the people you know are fooling around with cheap wastes of time and potential, like drinking, drugs, and casual sex. They figure they can clean up their act later after they've had their fill of fun. But God wants you to be paying attention right now—yes, at your age—remaining focused, staying constantly on the spiritual ball.

Knowing what you should do but not preparing yourself to do it may seem a lot easier on the frontside (verse 47), but it's a lazy attitude that's dead-on certain to bite you on the backside. Being alert to spiritual things now is the kind of life that promises blessing (verses 37-38,43).

Verse 48. We always want to know what'll happen to those who live in the middle of nowhere and die never hearing about Jesus. This verse hints at the answer—at the truth most believers know in their hearts—that God will deal fairly with everyone. In what's known as the "great white throne" judgment (Revelation 20:11-15), both the saved and the condemned are "judged according to their works." Final judgment, then, is apparently not a pass/fail proposition. Some of the unsaved will be "severely beaten" and others "beaten lightly." So . . . what we do with what we know on earth will matter in eternity.

12:49-53 War and Peace

Jesus came to bring us peace in our hearts. This was what He sent His followers out to proclaim (10:5). Yet His coming was bound to divide people into those who were either for or against Him. He left no room for riding the fence. "Peace I leave with you," He said—but not "as the world gives" (John 14:27). The world wants peace without a price. Jesus demands our all, yet promises peace that's even deeper.

Understand, though, that it is Jesus who does the dividing—not us. The Bible says, "If possible, on your part, live at peace with everyone" (Romans 12:18). Jesus is not giving us permission to be obnoxious with unbelievers or to disobey our parents and others in authority. People's problems should be with God, not with God's people.

12:54-59 Two More Teachings

Chapter 12 closes with a couple of warnings: *first*, not to be so hung up on trivial matters that we don't know God's word and His Spirit when we hear them; and *second*, not to let our little disputes and arguments fester until they take an act of Congress to sort out. Apologize. Clear the air. Jesus wants us to model His peace.

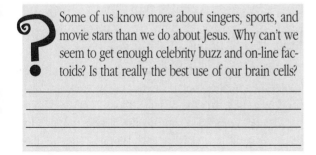

Some of us know more about singers, sports, and movie stars than we do about Jesus. Why can't we seem to get enough celebrity buzz and on-line factoids? Is that really the best use of our brain cells?

Luke 13

13:1-9 Life and Limb

Lessons from Tragedy (verses 1-5)

In any kind of tragedy, those who survive or watch it on the news may be just as worthy of death as those who die. Jesus taught that we are all on a crash course with tragedy, and only one thing can stop us from being ultimately destroyed: we all need to repent, to turn away from our sins and turn toward God.

In the two stories Jesus mentioned—which we know nothing else about—His audience had apparently concluded that the victims had gotten what they deserved. Repentance, though, and trust in Jesus is the only protection any of us have from final death.

Lessons from a Fig Tree (verses 6-9)

The same idea—our quickness to size up and cut down people who don't measure up to our standard—is also the theme of this follow-up parable. It's not that judgment is never going to occur, or that people are not going to have to stand before God and account for their sin. But Jesus is more willing than we are to keep weeding and watering and working in people's lives, hoping for better things.

13:10-17 A Straight-Up Miracle

The Scripture states that this woman was not just suffering from some sort of calcium deficiency but was actually "disabled by a spirit." Yet she was miraculously delivered from her demon oppression, apparently without asking. In doing so Jesus not only proved Himself "Lord of the Sabbath" (as He had in 6:1-11) but also exposed the hypocrisy of those who considered oxen and cattle more worthy of their attention than a woman in need of help. Always quick with a picky accusation, they were more con-

PILATE.
He was the Roman governor of Judea (A.D. 26—37) during Jesus' adult life. He demonstrated a serious lack of appreciation for Jewish religion and culture. His use of arrests and executions to put down a revolt among Samaritans resulted in his being recalled to Rome. Be watching for a lot more of him in chapter 23.

GALILEANS.
Galilee covered several cities in the northern part of the Holy Land, and those who lived there were known for being loose with the Jewish law (Acts 5:37), as well as for a noticeable speech accent that distinguished them from the Jews living around Jerusalem. Jesus Himself was a Galilean.

ABRAHAM.
Being a "daughter of Abraham" was just another way of saying that this woman was an Israelite. Abraham was the father of the Jews, called by God into this role way back in Genesis 12:1-3.

cerned about being proper than they were about helping people.

13:18-21 The Kingdom Is Like ...

Mustard Seed (verses 18-19)

Check out the size of one of these things next time you're in the spices at the grocery store. This tiny seed explodes into a fast-growing, treelike plant that can zoom as high as ten feet. God's kingdom is sort of like that—beginning with simple faith in Jesus, becoming a person whose life is transformed.

Yeast (verses 20-21)

Same thing goes for yeast. It takes such a tiny amount to make a whole loaf of bread rise into soft, delicious, help-yourself enjoyment. What's that wonderful aroma coming from God's kitchen? It's the heavenly smell of lives being changed from the inside out.

13:22-30 The Narrow Door

The man's question in verse 23 is (again) an attempt to compare and measure up—to see who's in and who's out in God's kingdom. But Jesus will not allow us to finger-point . . . except at ourselves. The question is not, "Are there few being saved?" The question is: Are you? Jesus' followers will come from everywhere—"from east and west, from north and south." But some who assume they're okay by tipping their hat to the "good Lord" every now and then may find out too late how good He really is.

SABBATH.
A day of rest and worship observed on the seventh day of the week. In Jesus' day religious tradition had attached hundreds of minor laws to the practice of Sabbath-keeping.

SYNAGOGUE.
The local meeting and assembly place for the Jewish people, close to what we'd think of as a church building.

KINGDOM PARABLES.
For an even bigger catalog of kingdom analogies, turn to Matthew 13:24-53.

ABRAHAM, ISAAC, JACOB.
These are known as the patri-archs of the Jewish religion—the fathers of the faith. They represent the first three generations of God's chosen people.

Verse 23. Is this what God wants—making sure that most people go to hell while few find their way to heaven? It's true that the concept of a Christian minority holds true throughout Scripture: God calling the tiny nation of Israel as His chosen people (Deuteronomy 7:7), as well as Jesus' statements that "many are invited, but few are chosen" (Matthew 22:14) and "there are many who go through" the gate of destruction (Matthew 7:13). But it's the hardness of people's hearts and the deception of sin that keeps people from believing (Hebrews 3:13), not the picky partiality of a small-time God.

Some students have made commitments to Christ in church services and on spiritual retreats and stuff, yet since then they haven't shown any evidence that they really meant it. What would Jesus say about them?

_____

_____

_____

_____

PROPHET.
This is someone who receives and declares a word from God. Jesus claimed to be a prophet and was recognized by others as one because of His powerful insight and teaching (John 4:19).

HISTORY.
Jerusalem. This was the chief city of Palestine—the name given to the land of the Bible (roughly modern-day Israel). The Jewish temple was there, and Jesus was crucified just outside its walls.

13:31-35 Jesus' Heart Breaks for Jerusalem

The Pharisees would have liked nothing better than to see Jesus shut up in seclusion. So their motivation for passing along Herod's threat was certainly not concern for Jesus' safety. But safety wasn't a big concern for Jesus either. Does He seem to be too worried about Herod?

However, His heart certainly broke over the people of Jerusalem, didn't it? Jesus said, "If you know Me, you will also know My Father" (John 14:7). Then take a good look at Jesus here. Those who see God as harsh and unmerciful need to see Jesus weeping over those who are lost. Does He sound to you like someone who doesn't care?

HALFTIME

We're a little past halfway through the Gospel of Luke, so it seems like a good time—especially in light of the "narrow door" we just talked about in chapter 13, as well as other passages that are coming up soon—to stop and make it really clear what God's salvation is all about.

Here's the History

The Bible says that all around us—in the predictability of the sunrise, in the return of springtime, in the papery precision of a wasp's nest, in a thousand million ways—is the idea that God is living, active, and real, "being understood through what He has made." This is called general revelation—the fact that God's "eternal power and divine nature" has been made known to everyone. "As a result, people are without excuse" (Romans 1:20).

But in Jesus, God has made Himself fully known. "He is the image of the invisible God" (Colossians 1:15). "He is the radiance of His glory, the exact expression of His nature, and He sustains all things by His powerful word" (Hebrews 1:3). Every promise made to us by God has been fulfilled in Jesus Christ. This special revelation we have received by getting to see, hear, and know the Son of God brings us face-to-face with Him—as well as with ourselves.

Here's the Deal

(1) *In light of His perfection, then, we find ourselves to be sinners* —"guilty" even before we were born; already "sinful" when our mothers conceived us (Psalm 51:5). "There is no one righteous, not even one" (Romans 3:10). "All have sinned and fall short of the glory of God" (Romans 3:23).

(2) *In light of His coming to earth, though, we find ourselves loved*—for when the time was just right, "God sent His Son, born of a woman, born under the law, to redeem those under the law, so that we might receive adoption as sons" (Galatians 4:4-5). "We love because He first loved us" (1 John 4:19).

(3) *In light of such grace, we find ourselves needing to repent and believe*—"'The message is near you, in your mouth and in your heart.' . . . If you confess with your mouth, 'Jesus is Lord,' and believe in your heart that God raised Him from the dead, you will be saved" (Romans 10:8-9).

(4) *So in light of His death—if we believe in Him—we will find ourselves forgiven*—"For rarely will someone die for a just person . . . but God proves His own love for us in that while we were still sinners Christ died for us" (Romans 5:7-8). "He has rescued us from the domain of darkness" and forgiven our sins (Colossians 1:13-14).

(5) *And in light of His resurrection—again, if we believe in Him—we can find ourselves unafraid*—for He has "abolished death and has brought life and immortality to light" (2 Timothy 1:10). "O Death, where is your victory? O Death, where is your sting?" We now have "victory through our Lord Jesus Christ" (1 Corinthians 15:55-57).

Jesus has done it all—lived a perfect life, died in our place, defeated death, and won for us an eternity with Him in heaven. The One who made us has come to save us . . . because He loves us.

What Do You Say?

If you're just now coming around to believing this for the first time, if you're ready to admit your need and to turn away from your sins—to turn toward a life that's way better than anything this world has to offer—then pray this prayer right now:

Lord God,

You have shown me today that I have no hope without you. I can't keep from sinning and messing up. It's part of who I am. And so I give up trying to make myself a better person. Instead, I need You to make me a new person. I confess my sins. I believe in You—in Your life, in Your death, in Your return from the grave. And I am ready to receive the salvation You have promised—a life of peace and joy on earth, a life of unending love with You forever. Come into my heart, Lord Jesus. I need You—now!

Luke 14

14:1-6 Return of the Sabbath Healer

This is very similar to the story in 13:10-16, where Jesus succeeded in both healing a woman on the Sabbath and driving the Pharisees into a sputtering rage. Only this time the religious experts could do nothing but stand speechless, unable to say much after Jesus' power and authority had done all His speaking for Him.

DROPSY.
Also called edema (ih-DEEM-uh), this disease can affect the heart, liver, kidneys, or brain, causing fluid retention and swelling throughout the body.

14:7-14 Party Etiquette

The Cheap Seats (verses 7-11)

Weddings aren't what you usually think of as places to learn humility, but Jesus said it would be a good place to practice it. The focus of a wedding, you know, is on the bride and groom. Yet plenty of the guests who show up are hoping other people will focus on them. Have you ever seen someone trying to draw attention to himself, only to end up looking obnoxious and out of place? Then you understand the universal principle Jesus lays down in verse 11: that "everyone who exalts himself will be humbled, and the one who humbles himself will be exalted." The best way to be thought highly of is to start by thinking more highly of others—and showing it in your actions and party manners.

OXEN.
Essential for farm work, these "beasts of burden" were often paired up to pull a plow or haul a load. Having one out of commission was like having your car broken down on the side of the road.

The Guest List (verses 12-14)

Jesus takes you from the wedding reception to the lunchroom—and asks you to look at the people sitting around your table. Is it always the same friends, people who have a lot of things in common with you, guys or girls you just easily get along with? Or do you ever sit down next to someone who's stuck over by themselves somewhere, who doesn't really have inroads into your kind of crowd, who you wouldn't naturally be drawn to for any reason other than that God loves them? To worry less about who

CONVERSATION.
The way Jesus used His context—a party—to talk about God's truth is a model for us to follow in bringing Christ up in conversation. Just about anywhere you are, no matter what people are talking about, there are natural ways to bring faith into play. Try it sometime. It's easier than you think.

you're seen with, and more about what you can do for somebody else, is one of the best ways to prove that your Christianity is more than skin deep, more than words, more than most people see in the lunchrooms of life.

Name a few of the people who'd be over at your house sometime if Jesus was making up the guest list. What kind of problems would that cause for you? What would keep you from following through on it?

_____

_____

_____

14:15-24 The Party of a Lifetime

Making Excuses (verses 18-20)

Jesus was still having dinner at one of the Pharisees' houses, so He continued to build teachings and parables around a party theme. The big event in this story was the "kingdom of God" banquet at the end of time. But then—as now—many don't think it's worth going to, even though it's the one party (you'd think) that no one would want to miss.

"Let Me tell you about the excuses I hear," Jesus said to His listeners. "People tell Me they're too busy, or they're not sure their date will like it, or they've got something else to do—something better has come along." And on and on it goes—spoiled rich kids trading in the invitation of a lifetime on temporary things that keep them too chained to the world.

Making Room (verses 21-24)

Jesus was trying to prepare His listeners' hearts to accept the fact that—surprise!—people you'd never expect to get God's invitation may be high on the guest list. Jesus called these the "poor, maimed, blind, and lame"—people who'd never be able to get there on their own, but by God's grace are welcomed right along with the others. In fact, to realize how "poor, maimed, blind, and lame" we all are is one of the first steps toward finding ourselves sitting next to Jesus rather than stuck forever outside.

WEDDING FEAST.
Throughout the New Testament, Christ and the church are seen in a marriage relationship—Jesus being the bridegroom, the church His bride (Ephesians 5:25-32). Heaven, then, will be the scene of a marriage feast between these two lovers, now eternally joined together (Revelation 19:6-9).

JEWS AND GENTILES.
The very idea that Gentiles (non-Jews) would ever be included in God's family was unthinkable to many Jews. In fact, it caused quite a blow-up in the early church, as seen at a big showdown at Jerusalem described in two biblical locations—Acts 15:1-35 and Galatians 2:1-10.

14:25-35 The High Cost of Christianity

Change of scenery. Jesus was on the road again, reminding the spectators and hang-arounders that if they really wanted to be part of what He was doing, they couldn't just be one of the groupies who came out for the show on the weekends. Living on the fringe is easy, but it's also empty. There's a better place—out on the edge with Jesus. It'll put your life on the line every day, but it'll give you the only life worth living.

That's why Jesus was willing to use a word like "cannot" without blinking an eye—as in, if you don't have a real love for Christ, if you're not willing to be His when it costs you, if you're not sure you can do without the things that separate you from Him, you "cannot be My disciple." It's that simple. The most miserable people in the world are those who try to build a Christian life with only a "foundation," not understanding that Jesus is going to want every room in the house. Miserable, too, are those who get caught up in the emotion of the moment and don't realize that Christianity is a real war against a real enemy. So the word for Christians is "good-bye" to the sidelines and hello to the battlefield.

SALT.
Zephaniah 2:9 talks about a "salt pit" that was probably located near the Dead Sea, an inland lake at the southern end of the Jordan River. The sodium chloride could sometimes leech out of the salt that crystallized in this area, leaving it with no taste whatsoever.

HEARING, LISTENING.
"Anyone who has ears to hear should listen!" [verse 35]. This is one of Jesus' frequent lines [Matthew 13:9,43, and more]—His way of explaining that He knew why some people didn't get the truth of what He was saying: because it wasn't what they wanted to hear.

Verse 26. Let me get this straight: Jesus wants me to love my enemies, but He wants me to "hate [my] own father and mother . . . brothers and sisters . . . even [my] own life"? If He just means we're supposed to love Him more than anyone else, why tell us to "hate" everybody we love? Surely He doesn't mean that! Well, He may mean that the love we have for Him should be so all-consuming that the love we have for our family and friends is like "hate" in comparison. But He's certainly trying to get across the idea that there's a huge cost to being a follower of Christ. It may take away from you everything you thought you could count on. It may put you at cross purposes with the people you love. You may have to hate what they stand for. This is serious business.

Luke 15

15:1-2 The Lost Crowd

Unpopular people. The ones nobody trusted. Cheaters and liars. Enemies of the Jewish religion. These made up the main audience for the three parables in this chapter. Yet amazingly, these "tax collectors and sinners" were interested enough in this Jesus to keep coming around, to keep wondering if this really was the Son of God.

SHEPHERDS.
The Bible mentions shepherds more than two hundred times—men who guarded, kept count, and took care of their flocks. The Bible also referred to kings and church leaders as shepherds who cared for the people under their authority.

RIGHTEOUS.
Being "righteous" is more than just being good. It means having the purity of God given to us. We are only clean in His eyes for one reason: Christ has died in our place and given us His righteousness (Philippians 3:9).

15:3-7 The Lost Sheep

This first parable is pretty easy to understand: the man in charge of the sheep (God) is responsible for all of them (His people). Not even one of us can straggle off without being noticed and gone after. Isn't it a little surprising, though, that the reaction in heaven to a lost person's rescue and salvation is much the same as the shepherd's celebration is described. The place must rock! That's how much God loves His people.

And don't think the "ninety-nine . . . who don't need repentance" are those who are good enough on their own, who made it in by obeying all the rules. They were just as lost as anybody else, but by God's grace they had been received into His family. They weren't perfect, but in one sense they had already been found, their salvation locked up tight.

15:8-10 The Lost Coin

Can you imagine losing a check for $500 in your room somewhere? You look for it and look for it. You blame everyone in your house for stealing it or moving it, perhaps for throwing it away accidentally. For days and days you hunt, you dig, you look in the same places over and over again; you try to remember. You can't believe what you've done! But a week later you find the check tucked inside an envelope you had set under some books. There it is! Your money is found! Now you know how the woman in this story feels.

Notice again the shared excitement that occurs when the lost item is found. It's what "friends and neighbors" are supposed to do—to "rejoice with those who rejoice" (Romans 12:15). It's what happens in heaven "over one sinner who repents." It's one of the things that makes God really happy: when someone receives His gift of salvation. Jesus seems to be saying to His listeners: "You need to rejoice over this, too. You need to get excited about the same things God is excited about."

> **?** When you hear of someone accepting Christ in your church or school, is it any big deal to you? If not, why? If so, what do you think the scene looks like in heaven the minute the angels get the good news?
>
> _____
>
> _____
>
> _____
>
> _____

SILVER COINS.
The lost coin was a drachma, a piece of Greek currency equal in value to the Roman denarius. It amounted to a day's wage for a common laborer.

GOD'S HEART.
Many people never see the delighted side of God's nature described in verses 7 and 10— nor in the upcoming parable of the lost son. For those who struggle to picture God as being anything other than harsh and indifferent, take them to these stories. Let them see the God who smiles.

15:11-32 The Lost Son

This parable is often called the "prodigal son"—prodigal meaning "reckless" or "wasteful"—which probably misses the point. Sure, any prodigal or potential prodigal could learn a lot here, but the star of this story is God, the gracious father.

Remember Jesus' main reason for telling these three parables? It wasn't to explain what missing sheep, coins, and little brothers are like. It was to tell what God is like, to beat back the criticism that Jesus was hanging around with sinners too much and seeming to enjoy their company. This story is way more about God than it is about us.

INHERITANCE.
According to ancient Jewish tradition, a father's possessions were handed down to his living sons—the oldest son getting a double portion.

FAMINE.
The Bible reports several famines [extreme shortages of food]—almost always caused by drought [long dry spells without rain]. Some famines lasted for years [Genesis 41:27], leaving people starved enough to eat garbage or even other humans. Famine was at times a direct judgment from God.

SLAVE VS. SON.
Read the opening verses of Romans, James, and Jude, and you'll see that all the greatest names of the New Testament considered themselves the "slave of God"—totally at the command of the Master. Though we too are to consider ourselves God's slaves [17:10], we are also God's children, bought out of slavery to sin and adopted into His heavenly family [Galatians 4:1-7].

The Rebellious Heart (verses 11-16)

Take a look at someone in full-on rebellion. He doesn't care about how his father feels or whether he'll lie awake at night worrying. He won't listen to authority, won't stop to think how his actions affect anyone else. He just wants to hang out with his friends, do whatever he likes, and treat the future like it's a million miles away. Some of what we imagine he did sounds alluring—the parties, the women, the nights on the town. But look how ugly it (always) turns. Keep your eyes on the end result—the barnyard, the hog slop. If you've been rebellious, you know how it feels. Deliberate sin will always lead us there eventually.

The Changed Heart (verses 17-19)

The two previous parables focused on the seeking love of God—a shepherd in search of his lost sheep, a woman on hands and knees hunting a missing coin. But a lost person is a little different. Unlike inanimate objects, he can be made to "[come] to his senses," turn around, and head for home. So like someone waking from a bad dream, this boy looked around and realized he messed up really bad. He sinned not only against his dad but against "heaven"—against God. He went back with little hope of ever being restored to his position in the family. He went home expecting to get the demotion he deserved. But he went anyway. That's all repentance really is—turning around and going home.

The Father's Heart (verses 20-24)

If you've ever run from God, this is the best news you've ever heard: the Father is running in your direction, His arms wide open, forgiveness written all over Him. You can give your canned apology if you want to, but don't be surprised if it's smothered in the warm embrace of His love and mercy. For you there's a new wardrobe, a hot meal, and an after-dinner party to follow. You'll have time later to talk about what you've learned and what kind of changes you need to make to keep this from happening again. But for now the ring and the robe await.

Repentance may seem like a big job on our end, but it's just the little part we play in God's grand love story between Father and child. Welcome home!

The Jealous Heart (verses 25-32)

Now for part two of this classic tale. The first half was told to show how God relates to the sinners and outcasts—with love, openness, and a willingness to save. This second part shows how God reacts to the self-righteous snobs who brought this subject up in the first place. Don't they see that their holier-than-thou sins of pride and petty jealousy are every bit as evil as a wild fling with potheads and prostitutes? Certainly, those who rebel against God in "foolish living" bring down "death" upon themselves. But those who think God doesn't have any business forgiving this kind of person don't know a thing about what it means to be "alive" in Him. They don't know how to "rejoice" over the things God loves.

FATTED CALF.
This was generally a young animal put up to be fed for slaughter. Often this meant that this calf was one of the strongest and choicest of the herd.

What are the rewards of obedience? What good things come to those who stay close to God all their lives? But what are the *dangers* of obedience? What bad things can grow in a religious heart that acts out of obligation but has no affection for the Father?

_____

_____

_____

_____

Luke 16

SHREWDNESS.
Many people think of Christians as wimpy doormats, but Jesus challenged His followers to be "shrewd as serpents" while remaining "harmless as doves" (Matthew 10:16). We are supposed to know how to handle ourselves in the real world without being corrupted by it (James 1:27).

WHOLE BIBLE.
When you come across a confusing passage like this, where the Bible seems to be saying something totally opposite to what it says in other places, don't try to build a case around one single verse. Take all the things the Bible says on the subject, lay them alongside each other, and ask the Holy Spirit to teach you what it all means. The Bible will never contradict itself. Approach it wanting to learn, not looking for loopholes.

16:1-9 Funny Money

Of all the parables Jesus told, this one may be the hardest to get. Here's a guy who's been accused of some kind of mismanagement of his master's money—whether by incompetence or laziness or (more likely) cooking the books, perhaps skimming some off the top for himself. His solution to being let go? Rather than confessing and promising to do better, he quickly started going to people who owed his boss money and discounted their bills by twenty to fifty percent. But hey—this isn't even his money! He's still cheating his employer for his own selfish benefit!

Verses 8-9. So why is the "master" praising the "unrighteous manager"? How does trying to save your own reputation at your boss's personal expense get high marks from Jesus? The only clue we get is that Jesus praised the man for acting "astutely"—shrewd, keen, discerning—for thinking on his feet. Notice that the guy is still called "unrighteous." Jesus isn't giving a total endorsement of his character. It's just that in this case, the filthy rascal took what little time and wiggle room he had left and made the most of it. It's a basic principle we all need to learn—to creatively use the tools of the world (money, work, relationships) to make inroads into other people's lives—only in our case, for eternal purposes. This seems to be the idea Jesus is setting up for the next few verses (10-12).

16:10-18 Money and Stuff

Handling It Wisely (verses 10-12)

Building off the last few words of verse 9, Jesus began to make clear that this story—in fact, most all His teaching—was really about eternity. While we're here on earth, we primarily have this-world things to deal with: homework, math tests, grass to cut, pizzas to deliver. If we focus on these just to get good grades and earn a paycheck, we miss the main point. These earthly things are not ends in themselves. They're really just a proving ground to show how ready we are to handle bigger things, more eternal things. They tell a lot about what's in our hearts and how serious we are about pleasing God.

The hearts of the Pharisees, of course, were big on wanting power and control—now!—in this world— yet it was precisely their preoccupation with this world, their greed and shortsightedness, that kept them from enjoying the influence they wanted. God wouldn't give them something "genuine"—the ability to think eternally, to lead others with godly authority—when they hadn't even been faithful with what He'd given them already—like their stupid money, for example. They didn't understand that eternity had started happening already in their everyday lives, with everyday things.

Holding It Loosely (verse 13)

Do you know people who always seem to be short of money, who are always asking to borrow a few dollars from you? Then you know some people who *love* money, who are so addicted to material things that they can't control their buying reflex.

Money, Jesus said, has the power to enslave—a power we routinely underestimate. When getting money (and the things that *come* with money) is what turns us on, it's like a toggle switch that shuts off our passion for following Christ. It's simply impossible to "be devoted to one" without "despis[ing] the other."

LITTLE THINGS.
You're going to see this same principle again in Jesus' parable from 19:11-27—that those who are "faithful in a very small matter" are the ones who are entrusted with bigger things.

GREED.
Money is called "unrighteous" in this chapter because it's a worldly item, but not because it's inherently bad. Money itself is neither good nor evil. Yet the greed that stinks all around it is so strong. God calls the love of money "a root of all kinds of evil" (1 Timothy 6:10).

Keeping It in Perspective (verses 14-15)

The Pharisees came under the knife again, their motives exposed by a God who "knows [their] hearts," who knew they had convinced themselves that money was evidence of God's favor, not a false god threatening to take His place. Again, you see a group of religiously minded people who are out of step with the God they claimed to serve. By valuing the same things the world does, they placed little stock in the things that interested God and therefore became "revolting" in His sight. That's a scary place to be.

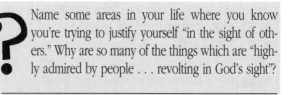

Name some areas in your life where you know you're trying to justify yourself "in the sight of others." Why are so many of the things which are "highly admired by people . . . revolting in God's sight"?

_____

_____

_____

_____

LAW AND PROPHETS.
What we now know as the Old Testament was, of course, the full Bible to those living during Jesus' time. It was made up of five books of Law (Genesis—Deuteronomy) plus the Prophets and the Writings. "The Law and the Prophets," then, was their way of saying "the Bible."

16:16-18 Legal Proceedings

First, Jesus answered His critics who claimed that His radical ideas flew in the face of the teachings of Scripture. Quite the opposite. Jesus defended every word of God—down to the last letter—and He loved it more dearly and was obeying it more completely than those who said they knew it better than He did. He had not abandoned the law of God; He was living it right before their eyes—whether they liked the way it looked or not.

DIVORCE.
The Bible's teachings on divorce are heavily debated these days, especially since so many families have been touched by it. To read the longest passages that deal with divorce and other marriage issues, turn to Matthew 19:3-9 as well as the whole seventh chapter of 1 Corinthians.

Then, as if to prove His point, He reminded the Pharisees how they had twisted a certain passage of Scripture (Deuteronomy 24:1-4) to mean they could divorce their wives on the grounds of bad breath or something (Matthew 5:31). Marriage in God's sight was far more valuable than they were treating it. To dissolve a marriage is a serious offense against God and each other.

16:19-31 Heaven and Hell

This parable is a little different from all the others because Jesus actually used people's names in it. Could it be, then, that this is more than just an object lesson—that this is a true story? Either way, the picture of heaven is certainly true: the angelic escort, the end of suffering, the reunion with the family of God. So is the picture of hell: bitter, burning torment, separated from those you love, made worse by being able to see into paradise at the same time.

The appearance of "Abraham" (the father of Israel; national and religious hero rolled into one) as well as "Moses and the prophets" tied into Jesus' comments from previous verses, further cementing His connection with the law and with the roots of Jewish faith. He was telling His listeners that He was the Son of the same God they knew and talked about, not some new religious wacko out fishing for converts.

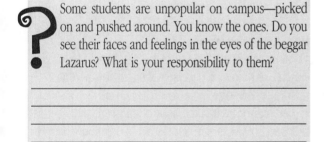

Some students are unpopular on campus—picked on and pushed around. You know the ones. Do you see their faces and feelings in the eyes of the beggar Lazarus? What is your responsibility to them?

_____

_____

_____

_____

HEAVENLY BODIES?

Notice all the body parts mentioned in this after-death experience: Abraham's side, as well as the rich man's eyes, finger, and tongue. To find out more about what our bodies will be like after we die, visit 1 Corinthians 15:35-49.

HADES.

This is the realm of the dead. The same word in Hebrew, the language of the Old Testament, is sheol, which is often described as a place of suffering but also as a netherworld for all those who have died.

ON TO HEAVEN?

Some believe that when we die, we go into sort of a holding tank or a sleeplike state, waiting for the final judgment. Granted, there are mysteries about what our experience will be like after death, but the clear teaching of this parable as well as other passages (like John 12:26, 2 Corinthians 5:8, Philippians 1:23) is that as soon as we are "out of the body," we will be "at home with the Lord."

17:1-10 More Jesus Teachings

Do As I Do? (verses 1-2)

MILLSTONES.
These were two circular stones that spun against one another to grind grain into flour. Each stone was usually 2 to 4 inches thick and about a foot and a half in diameter, made of basalt and heavy as all get-out.

Leading other people into sin is serious business with Jesus. Those who use peer pressure to force someone into a compromising situation, or who tempt someone sexually, or who set a poor example of behavior for younger kids, are warned ahead of time that God is aware when this kind of bullying and egging on is happening.

So as Jesus turned back to his disciples, giving them some warnings and instructions, He included this one: others are watching, so be careful what you're doing. Sure, everyone is ultimately responsible for his or her own actions (Galatians 6:5), but we each have a hand in either leading others to Christ or standing in their way, causing them to stumble. And God will hold us accountable for how we handle that responsibility.

ACCOUNTABILITY.
If anyone thinks they're free to do whatever they want without regard for how it might affect somebody else, take them to Romans 14. It's probably the clearest Bible passage on the subject.

Hard to Forgive (verses 3-6)

Think of someone who just makes life miserable for you. How do you forgive a person like that for the things he does to you or says about you? Tough, isn't it?

But forgiveness is at the heart of Christian faith. The disciples sort of got this. When Jesus told them how high His demand for forgiveness was—"seven times in a day" and *more* if necessary!—they thought they needed an "increase" in faith in order to do that. But just as God's forgiveness of us was what first gave us faith in Him, our daily forgiveness of others will result in our faith getting deeper. See, faith isn't something we store up waiting for a chance to use. Faith is something that grows on the back of our obedience—and rarely faster than when we give others the gift of our forgiveness, just as God did for us.

Verse 6. But if we have enough faith, can we pretty much tell God what we want . . . and expect it to happen? And if it doesn't happen, does it mean we just don't have enough faith, not even a "mustard seed" full? No, the issue isn't about having *more faith*—or more of *anything* that has to do with us. Faith is all about trusting in a big God—a God who's wise and powerful enough to know exactly what He needs to do and exactly what we most need to have happen. God wants us to think bigger than mustard seeds and mulberry trees. He wants us to be so full of Him that all we want is what He wants.

Just Doing My Job (verses 7-10)

This issue of "big God, little us" gets really honest here, when Jesus gave this quick example of a servant preparing a meal for his master. The owner's ingratitude may have seemed a bit insensitive to our ears. We expected him to sympathize with his slave a little bit, maybe even have him pull up a chair and join him. But the servant knew his place. It's pride alone that can make us see more in ourselves than is really there.

17:11-19 Am Thankful or Amnesia?

The lepers stood at a distance—(they always did . . . their rank, disgusting skin disorder making them impure and unclean, dangerously contagious). Do you know people who stand at a distance? People who are unpopular? People with some form of disability? Know what, though? Even people who stand at a distance can be arrogant. Just because they're treated badly by others doesn't mean that in their own hearts they can't have the same seeds of hatred and discrimination. Sometimes those who are outcasts can harbor such resentment and bitterness, their spirits are just as polluted as those who mistreat them.

REBUKE.
This is a reprimand, a serious challenge, very blunt and honest —right to someone's face, not behind her back or even through innocent "prayer request"-style gossip. Rebukes take courage; but just like forgiveness, they're a "must" to living a free, transparent, no-nonsense Christian life.

SAMARITANS.
These were people from the central Israelite region of Samaria, many of whom were the children of intermarriages with non-Jewish colonists from the invading Assyrians. This created huge racial and ethnic hostilities between the Samaritan half-breeds who were hated by the Jews returning to their homeland from exile in Babylon.

PRIESTS.
Jesus' instructions for the lepers to "show [them]selves to the priests" dated back to the Old Testament law, described in Leviticus 14:1-32.

Apparently, nine of the ten lepers in this story felt entitled to their healing. They felt like they had gotten back what was rightfully theirs to begin with—a healthy body, a place in the community. This kind of pride and self-centeredness forms one of the underlying themes of this chapter: pride that threatens to make us uncaring toward others (verse 2), unable to forgive (verse 4), unwilling to submit to God's authority (verse 10) . . . and unaware that we need to say "thank you, God" a whole lot more than we do.

> What do you think when you do something for somebody else but they show no gratitude? How do you think the Father feels about those who receive so much from Him but don't bother to recognize it?
>
> _____
> _____
> _____
> _____

KINGDOM OF GOD.
It's not a place or a country. It's the rule of God over history and all eternity. His rule in the lives of people who are submitted to His authority. It's a present reality in the hearts of believers today, yet is waiting for its full expression when all its subjects are gathered together in heaven.

17:20-37 Kingdom Come

Present Tense (verses 20-21)

The Pharisees weren't looking for the kind of kingdom Jesus was talking about—God's unseen rule in His people's hearts—but for something much more visible and immediate: a political kingdom to throw off Roman oversight of their homeland and reestablish Jewish self-government. Christ's kingdom, though, was already "among" them by virtue of His presence, a kingdom that exists beyond time and national borders, a kingdom that can thrive in the midst of any circumstances or situation.

Future Tense (verses 22-25)

Jesus spoke again to His disciples—those who were more likely to understand the deeper meaning of His kingdom—telling them not to expect God's rule to come the way most people would anticipate it. When you see it, Jesus said, you'll know it—like "lightning flashes" in the sky. This refers to His second coming—the future aspect of His kingdom—a final victory made possible only by the death of the King's Son.

Very Tense (verses 26-37)

We again see Jesus not merely as King but also as a prophet, accurately forecasting what some of the moods and events will be like as His final kingdom approaches: people going about their business, oblivious to God's greater plans and His warnings of coming judgment.

The stories of Noah and Lot are particularly appropriate, because both men received news of approaching events that seemed impossible to believe—a worldwide flood and a major city's destruction—yet they listened to what God was saying, did what He commanded, and found themselves safely separated from those who thought it was a big joke.

Notice also another unexpected example of kingdom thinking (verse 33). Looking for a totally safe place in this world is a waste of time. Our lives are in God's big, capable hands. When we lose our lives there, we find all they were ever meant to be. We find the only security that's really available to us.

 Verses 34-36. Is this a snapshot of what will happen at the return of Christ? Certainly this is part of it. But the main point of Jesus' words was not to describe the endless details of end-times action but to warn people to be prepared for His sure and certain return, for the absolute reality of His coming kingdom.

DAY OF THE LORD.
This was an Old Testament synonym for God's judgment and deliverance, which the New Testament writers deepened to mean Christ's final coming—the ultimate judgment day.

SON OF MAN.
This name for Jesus not only expressed His humanity but is also the title most associated with His return to earth and His judgment of humanity.

NOAH AND LOT.
The story of Noah and the ark is found in Genesis 6—8. The story of Lot and his family's escape from Sodom comes from Genesis 18:16—19:29. Lot's wife turned around to see the city in flames (disobeying God's direct command) and was turned into a salt statue. Some people won't listen.

Luke 18

ELECT.

These are the people of God, who have entered into special relationship with Him through His Son, Jesus Christ. They have been known by Him "before the foundation of the world" [Ephesians 1:4] and will remain His possession throughout all eternity.

18:1-8 The Prayer Nagger

The haunting scenes from the closing half of chapter 17 have left a noticeable look of worry and fear on the faces of Jesus' followers. So you can almost see the reassurance in His face as He tells this parable. Yes, in many ways we are helpless, much like the widows in Jesus' day. But the widow could beg for mercy. She could nag even a merciless judge to hear her appeal for justice. And so can we.

But just like His parable from 11:5-8, Jesus was not saying that God greets us with the rolled-eyes, cigar-chomping anger of a crusty official or a grumpy neighbor. He was just saying that if even grouchy guys like these can be pestered and persuaded into helping us, what should we expect from a God who loves us and cares about what happens to us? With faith in Him, our hope is secure.

18:9-14 The Prayer of the Humble

Jesus asked (verse 8) whether He would find anyone with genuine "faith on earth." If He does, they will look like the tax collector in this story, not the other guy with his do-good pride and arrogance, basking in his own self-esteem. The funny thing (pitiful, really) is that the Pharisee in this parable would be the last person to suspect that his brand of religion didn't put him high on God's list of playmakers. Let his blindness be a warning to you—never to have anything shining in your eyes but Jesus Christ.

Verse 11. What's so bad about being someone who's not "greedy, unrighteous" or any of the other things on the Pharisee's list of promotional credits? Isn't that what God wants from us—to avoid doing bad things, to be serious about our disciplines, to put our money in the offering plate, to be really good Christians? Of course. But not so we can stack our pile of good deeds up before Him, convincing Him what a good find He made in us— and especially not to compare ourselves with how others are doing! What God is looking for is a heart that knows how dependent we are on Him for everything.

PHARISEES.
They were the largest and most influential of the three major Jewish parties, controlling the synagogues and holding people to the strictest letter of the law—or at least to their interpretation of it. The term literally means "separated ones," based on their practice of pulling away from other people to study and debate.

TAX COLLECTORS.
These were usually government agents of Rome, though sometimes they were Jewish men working against their own people, responsible for gathering [and often inflating the amount of] tax money due from people in their provinces. Kind of the lowest of the low. Right down there with the prostitutes.

18:15-17 The Blessing of the Children

As a living picture to illustrate one of His main teachings— that "everyone who exalts himself will be humbled, but the one who humbles himself will be exalted" (verse 14)— Jesus rebuked His disciples for thinking that they and the other grown-ups were the only ones worthy of being near Him, of making demands on His time. Jesus saw—and He wanted them to see—that the joyful, innocent awe which spread freely over the faces of these kids meant more to Him than all the good deeds in the world done for no other purpose than being noticed. It's a liberating humility we can never afford to outgrow.

18:18-23 The Rich, Young Ruler

Why did this man call Jesus "good"? Because he had seen Jesus going around doing good things? Probably. At least that seems to be how this guy defined his *own* goodness— by not being sexually immoral or hateful or corrupt or mean to anybody. But he didn't understand that "good" and "people" are two words that can never really go together. "No one is good but One—God."

His other problem was that he didn't really come to Jesus for help and advice, only for approval—an approval he never received because he didn't want the goodness Jesus had come to offer. We should never go to God wanting anything but the truth, because that's all He'll ever give us.

Verse 22. When Jesus told this guy to "sell all that you have and distribute it to the poor," was He just exaggerating for emphasis, or is this really what He expects from all of us? Well, it would seem pointless of the Bible to teach us about being good managers of our money if what God really wanted was for us to give it all away. The only thing we know *for sure* from this story is that He told *this particular individual* to do that. Jesus knew that money and stuff were the real gods in this guy's life, so He challenged him at the heart of his idol. What is your idol? And what does God tell *you* to do about it in order to come clean from it?

IMPOSSIBLE?

Jesus' reminder in verse 27 is the same assurance the angel Gabriel gave to Mary back in 1:37, after he told her she would be the mother of Christ. Truly, "nothing will be impossible with God."

18:24-30 Giving Much, Getting More

"Then who can be saved?" If a good guy like this rich, young ruler can't get in, if people with money can't get in, then who's left? Only the people who have nothing to hold onto except their faith in God. People who love Him even more than they love their parents, their family, and the people who are closest to them. People who have traded in the small-time pleasures of earthly living for the matchless rewards of "eternal life." This goes for everybody. "There is no one" who puts all their eggs in God's basket who won't find life on earth richer and fuller and will then find life with Him forever and ever.

18:31-34 No Crown without a Cross

For the third time (also in 9:22 and 9:44), Jesus pulled His closest followers away privately to tell them the bitter secret of God's plan: it's going to require His gut-wrenching death. Don't zip past the mental images: "mocked, insulted, spit on," followed by beatings, floggings, death. But the full force of it still seemed lost on His disciples, who weren't ready yet to grasp it. However, it was important that Jesus say it anyway, though, because when they'd look back, months and years down the road, they'd remember, "That Jesus! Everything He said came true, even when it cost Him His life. Why should I doubt Him now?"

Have you ever had something happen to you, and it brought back to mind some advice your parents had given you or a verse you'd read in the Bible? And you thought, "Oh yeah, now I get it!"

_____

_____

_____

DEATH PROPHECY.
See if you can spot some of the actual details of Jesus' death foretold in terrifying, poetic colors —hundreds of years in advance —in places like Psalm 22 and Isaiah 53.

18:35-43 The Healing of the Blind Man at Jericho

Prayer is how this chapter started, and prayer is how it ends—not the eyes-closed, hands-folded kind, but the desperation, don't-stop-me-now, I've-got-to-see-Jesus kind of praying we're usually too smug to spit out. Just as in the parable of the widow and the unjust judge (18:1-8), God responds to the pesky, nagging beggar who's not too proud to stand alone—who's quick to give all the glory to God.

NAZARENE.
Jesus was born in Bethlehem, but His growing-up years were spent in Mary and Joseph's hometown of Nazareth, just as the prophets had said (Matthew 2:23).

SON OF DAVID.
Jesus was the son of Joseph, you remember, but in a larger context He was the descendent of David, the greatest king ever in Israel. Jesus was the ultimate "chosen one" to lead God's people.

19:1-10 Zacchaeus

How would you like to change your reputation? You might be surprised how many people would. If you're one of them, you'll enjoy getting to know Zacchaeus, because Jesus gave Him an incredible opportunity to do just that. He can do it for you, too.

Jericho was a wealthy city, fed by an underground spring that made it a "city of palms" (Deuteronomy 34:3) and the winter capital for Herod the Great, complete with palaces, baths, and gardens—a spring-like oasis in the Middle Eastern desert. So Zacchaeus wasn't the only rich man who lived there—just one who proved that a rich man can go through "the eye of a needle" (18:25), although you'll hardly recognize him on the other side.

Again, Jesus was willing to be seen in public not just with someone accused of having a bad reputation, but someone who deserved every word of it. That's because Jesus knew these were the people who needed to be with Him the most—to see themselves for who they really were, to desire to be somebody different, to want to be like Him. Jesus is truly a reputation changer. He's the one who seeks us before we even know we're lost. Verse 10 is a big theme verse that captures Christ's mission in a nutshell.

RESTITUTION.
The restoring of stolen, lost, or damaged property was part of the Old Testament law (Exodus 22:1-15) and is also a proper response to our own salvation, making amends to others for the sins we've committed (Ezekiel 33:14-16).

COMMON GRACE.
This is the idea that all people —not just believers—are given blessings and gifts from God. Every good thing that comes into any person's life is a result of the goodness of God.

19:11-27 Playing Games with God

Some people like to play around with God, to try seeing how little they can get away with doing, to see how close they can skirt the gray areas. But one thing we learn about God's character (through the "nobleman" in this story) is that He is very *demanding*. Boy, that's something you don't hear very often! Many people today think of God as a big pushover, a teddy bear who'll say "aw, that's OK" to any little excuse or apology. But like this king, God *expects* something from us—a return on His investment, something to show for the gifts He's given—like our intellect or athletic ability or personality. He wants these things multiplied, exercised, and put to work. Just ask the guy in verses 20-24 if He found God a force to be reckoned with!

Notice also that everyone is given a different skill set—some are even given more than others—but each person is responsible just for the ones he has, not for what he has in comparison to someone else.

Another big point is that just because some people don't "want" God to "rule over" them doesn't mean that He won't. God is the ruler over everyone, whether they like it or not. But look at the blessing and reward He gives to those who choose to *embrace* His rule rather than feel imposed upon by it.

MINA.
Originally a unit of weight equivalent to a little over a pound, the mina later became a unit of currency equal to about three month's wages. The talent (used in a similar parable from Matthew 25:14-30) was worth even more—as much as $1,000.00.

19:28-40 Jesus' Final Week Begins

This "triumphal entry" into Jerusalem (as it's often called) is the event we celebrate on Palm Sunday, one week before Easter. Watch the crowds continue to grow as Jesus descended the Mount of Olives, riding bravely toward His destiny. His admirers were shouting a praise from Psalm 118:26, much to the dismay of the Pharisees, who continued to the end to be threatened by the way He captivated people's hearts.

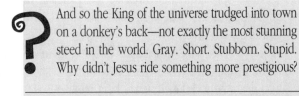

And so the King of the universe trudged into town on a donkey's back—not exactly the most stunning steed in the world. Gray. Short. Stubborn. Stupid. Why didn't Jesus ride something more prestigious?

_____

_____

_____

THE DONKEY.
Jesus' choice of a donkey for His ride into Jerusalem was prophesied in Zechariah 9:9.

MOUNT OF OLIVES.
Jesus' return to earth a second time will also come by way of this mountain, as dramatically foretold in Zechariah 14:4-9.

19:41-44 Jesus' Heart Shows Through

If a mike had been placed on the donkey's back, here's what you would have heard Jesus saying as he neared Jerusalem: It wouldn't have been curses on the Pharisees, or fear for His life, or self-pity over His fate. Instead it would have been tear-filled words of compassion for those who had been so close to God's presence yet so blind to His love and purposes.

Yes, there would come a day—a generation later in A.D. 70—when Rome would crush a Jewish uprising in Jerusalem and "not leave one stone on another." (Jesus said more about this in 21:20-24.) And it hurt Him to think about their suffering. Could any of us have been that concerned about others . . . when our own tortured death was only a few hours away . . . and we already knew every painful detail of it?

THE TEMPLE.
Jesus' words in verse 46 come from Isaiah 56:6-7 and Jeremiah 7:9-11. This event (as well as John the Baptist's ministry) is also interestingly predicted in Malachi 3:1-4.

LEADERS.
The Jewish leaders were singled out for their part in the plot over Jesus' death. That's because leaders are held to a higher level of accountability for what they lead others to do (James 3:1).

19:45-48 What Happens to Weak Leaders

This whole event showed the poor leadership that existed in Israel's ruling classes—like the chief priests (political figureheads), scribes (religious teachers), and other elder statesmen. As it always does, bad leadership had filtered its way down to the people, resulting in a fake, insincere obedience to rules and regulations. But Christ's authentic authority was changing people's hearts, exposing holes in their pointless practices, and revealing the paranoia of those whose leadership was weak and selfish—and were now out to get this Jesus!

The scene of merchants selling birds and livestock to the people who were coming to the temple to make sacrifices was not a surprise to Jesus. It would be a mistake to say that He blew up, that His temper tantrum was an over-the-top sign of stress. He had come to restore genuine faith and religion to the temple—to God's people—to turn the tables on those who were turning the people's need and desire to worship into pure profiteering.

Luke 20

20:1-8 Who Died and Made You Boss?

Working hard to build a case against Jesus, grilling Him in the court of public opinion, the Jewish leaders decided to go with a trip-up line of questioning. Did Jesus seem knocked off balance by their tactics or in any way rattled by their potential to do Him harm? Hardly. Jesus was *their* authority, and He *knew* it. They had appointed themselves to positions of authority in fulfillment of their own wishes. But God Himself had given authority to Jesus (and John the Baptist, who showed up again in this passage) in fulfillment of divine prophecy.

QUESTIONS.
This also came up in chapter 9. When people tried to trap Jesus with questions, one way He responded to them was to come back with a question. If someone wants to play mind games with you over religion, this is a good way to tell if they really want answers or are just being smart-alecks.

20:9-19 Whose Blood Is on Your Hands?

Rather than name names and point fingers, Jesus chose to tell a parable to prepare people for what was about to happen to Him. It's a method that brilliantly communicated His meaning to those who wanted to understand while confounding those who refused to listen.

The "slaves" in verses 10-12 are the Old Testament prophets, many of whom were killed for daring to speak God's truth in the face of human greed and ambition. The "beloved son," of course, is Jesus, sent to gather His father's harvest from the "tenant farmers" (the Jewish leaders) who had been left in charge of caring for God's people and maintaining the integrity of the faith. But these leaders didn't love what the Father loved. And their destruction at His hand would be what they rightfully deserved. Any fool could see that—any fool but the ones who were starting to get the message that He knew what they were up to.

PROPHETS.
One of the prophets who endured repeated persecution at the hands of the people was Jeremiah, who was threatened with death (Jeremiah 26:7-15), thrown into jail (37:11-16), and tossed into an empty, muddy well (38:1-6).

THE CORNERSTONE.
Find this early reference to Jesus' death and rejection in Psalm 118:22.

FLATTERY.
False flattery looks as ugly now as it did in verse 21. Read more about its slick-hearted dangers in Proverbs 26:28, 28:23, and 29:5.

20:20-26 A Question about Taxes

Now the religious leaders were doing anything—*a-ny-thing!*—to trap Jesus in a slip of the tongue, resorting to unethical activity in order to justify their "righteous" assignment. They thought they had found their issue—the controversial poll tax which so angered the Jews. They resented having to use the special Roman coin reserved for that purpose, which was engraved with the likeness of the emperor. So Jesus could have raised Jewish eyebrows by coming out in support of the tax. But if He spoke out against it, He would have been guilty in the eyes of the state. Arrestable. Yep, they thought they had Him. But they thought wrong. The spinners of words had met their match in the Spinner of the heavens.

> What do you think Jesus means in verse 25? Where do the lines get fuzzy between our twin obligations of being good citizens of our country as well as true citizens of heaven?
>
> _____
>
> _____
>
> _____

20:27-40 A Question about Doctrine

Another stupid, spider-web question. Hypothetical hooey. Yet Jesus, who had enough on His mind as it was, was still listening to people's requests, still responding to His challengers, still fulfilling everything the Father had demanded of Him.

This peek into heaven reveals a place where marriage is not so much forbidden as it is unnecessary. Heaven will be at full capacity the moment final judgment is complete. And one of the main businesses of marriage—conceiving and bearing children—will no longer be needed. Instead, the church will be married to Christ (Revelation 19:7) just as we are symbolically married to Him on the earth (Ephesians 5:22-32).

In short, Jesus was telling His accusers that there were bigger, deeper concepts at work than the shallow spiritual water most people were satisfied swimming in. "Read the Bible for yourself," He seemed to be saying in verses 37-38, "and see that God is both awesome and eternal."

Verse 36. Are we going to be angels when we get to heaven? The wings, the halos, the whole bit? Well, the halos and all were added by artists and painters, way after the Bible had already told us everything we needed to know about angels. But Jesus' comment that we will be "like angels" after we die means—(when you read it in context)—that we will be like them in at least this one aspect: we will never die. Don't take it much further than that.

20:41-44 A Question about David

There being no further questions (verse 40), Jesus took the opportunity to ask one Himself. Many were looking for a Messiah (an "anointed" or "chosen one") who would ascend like King David to an earthly throne, restoring the nation of Israel to its Old Testament glory. But Jesus turned to words familiar to His listeners (Psalm 110:1) to show them that their great King David himself, the writer of this very Psalm, recognized that he was outclassed by Israel's coming Ruler. Jesus was all that and more.

20:45-47 The End of All Questions

In words very similar to His warnings in Matthew 6:1-18, Jesus said what others could only whisper around their breakfast tables: that the religious professionals of their day were showboats and shysters. But these guys' chickens were coming home to roost . . . in the bloody trail of judgment reserved for those who peddle God's Word for pleasure and profit.

BURNING BUSH.
You'll remember this story from Exodus 3:1–4:17, where God called Moses to the mission of leading the children of Israel out of slavery in Egypt.

SADDUCEES.
This was another party in Jewish society——like the Pharisees, though these two groups differed sharply. The Sadducees (SAD-you-sees) were made up primarily of rich aristocrats who claimed to be descendents of Zadok, the high priest during Solomon's reign. They were what's called materialists, not believing in life after death, in spiritual beings like angels and demons, or in a very active, living God of any sort.

SCRIBES.
Mostly Pharisees, these were experts on Jewish history and tradition, responsible for teaching it to others and serving as star witnesses in cases where a ruling on the law of Moses was in question.

Luke 21

GIVING.
Sacrificing time, money, and comfort for another person is something today's students are pretty good at. So, use this current wave of crisis causes to show God's love to the hurting. Get out there with others who don't share your faith, and show them the reason why Christians care.

21:1-4 A Poor Woman's Offering

There's a teaching going around today that says, "The more God blesses you (with money and things, primarily), the more God must love you." Well, here's a good passage to prove that this "health and wealth gospel" (as it's called) is so misguided.

Funny, isn't it, that Jesus didn't choose to brag on a rich man in this little sidelight event. Or that He didn't condemn this woman for her poverty and her (obvious) lack of faith. No, His message is pretty simple: God is not impressed by the dollar amounts of our offerings. He's much more concerned with the level of our sacrifice, with how much of our full weight we're willing to trust into His care, depending on Him for our full supply. Money has its place in our lives, but not as a measuring stick for God's approval.

21:5-6 The Destruction of the Temple

"Uh, you guys are not listening." No sooner had Jesus finished praising the poor widow for her sacrifice than a little group of patriotic Palestinians started patting themselves on the back for their nation's beautiful temple. These people may not have had a lot of money of their own, but they loved being associated with someone or something that did. You know how it feels to be acquainted with an important person or to be part of a school with a successful sports team? Well, here these people were, enjoying being on the fringes of greatness, overly impressed with exteriors and fleeting appearances.

Yet with the same drastic word picture He painted in 19:44, Jesus began His prophecy of Jerusalem's destruction—beginning with this temple they took such pride in—much the same way as the prophet Jeremiah had done hundreds of years before (Jeremiah 7:12-15). Sure enough, the original temple was sacked by the Babylonians around 587 B.C. And the temple of Jesus' day would meet the same ill fate at the hands of the Romans. His prophecy was always dead on.

21:7-11 The Beginning of the End

"When?" We all want to know the answer to that question. "When will these things be"—these signs of the end times? The rest of this chapter is a broad-brush description of two future events: the fall of Jerusalem (which was still in the future at this time) and the end of the world. So be sure not to confuse the two. Verses 8-24 seem to talk more about the first, verses 25-36 about the second.

The people in verse 7 mainly wanted to know about the first one, specifically when the temple was going to be torn down, as Jesus was predicting. True to form, He wasn't as concerned about dates and headlines as He was about people's hearts, those who were in danger of being "deceived" during this unsettling season. The days ahead were going to be hard, but He would be their anchor in the storm.

TWO-SIDED PROPHECY.
Bible prophecy often deals with two different events: one in the near future and another more distant. Obadiah, for example, could truthfully say in verse 15 of his book: "the day of the LORD is near"—God's judgment on a pressing matter—while also meaning that God's final "day" was still to come.

21:12-19 Tough Times Ahead

Targeted for suspicion. Tossed into jail. Hauled before trial courts. Beaten into submission. Kicked out of their houses. Cruel names spit into their faces. This was what Christ's followers had to look forward to over the following years as Jerusalem prepared to be ransacked. They would experience punishment from the Roman state and persecution from their own families and countrymen. So Jesus gave them three things to remember: (1) endure it—it will be worth the cost, (2) proclaim it—I will give you the words, (3) believe it—I will protect you down to the last hair on your head. *Even in death, I will take care of you.*

WITNESSING.
Talking to others about Jesus, especially when you're under the gun and under pressure, is a job that calls for the Holy Spirit. It's something you have to be willing to stick your neck out and do, but once you're out there, you'll find that He's with you.

How do you think you would have made it during this time of intense persecution? What kinds of trials and troubles could come into your life today and threaten to derail you from walking with Christ?

_____

_____

_____

MASADA.
Another fascinating story that followed on the heels of Jerusalem's fall was the Roman siege on the desert fortress at Masada (Muh-SAH-duh), where nearly 1,000 Jewish men, women, and children chose suicide rather than be taken by the Roman armies.

21:20-24 Jerusalem to Fall

There comes a time to run for your lives. And this would be it, Jesus told them: "when you see Jerusalem surrounded by armies." Beginning in A.D. 66 (somewhere between 30 and 40 years after Jesus was saying this), the Romans were at the gates as the Jews began openly resisting the foreign occupation of their homeland. By A.D. 70 the Jews had literally fallen "by the edge of the sword" and been "led captive into all the nations"—their temple torched, their country in ruins and enemy hands, their survivors and sacred artifacts paraded as trophies through the streets of Rome—just like Jesus said.

REDEMPTION.
To redeem someone meant to pay whatever price was needed to buy the release of a convicted criminal. God sent Jesus to pay our price, to set us free, to give us redemption from our sins.

21:25-28 And That's Not All

The terrifying fall of the great city of Jerusalem would be simply one of many horrors to grip humanity in the centuries since Jesus spoke these words. Even today, "fear and expectation of the things that are coming on the world" are constantly in the papers and on the public's radar. Truly, the whole order of creation is wearing down, decaying, showing signs of just how temporary it really is. So Jesus began helping His followers look beyond the immediate, beyond A.D. 70, down the years to a day when He would be seen again "coming in a cloud," His power and "great glory" raining from the skies, ultimate relief so close they could taste it.

21:29-33 The Parable of the Fig Tree

Now Jesus seemed to be speaking in general terms—about both coming events—giving His followers enough warning not to be surprised by either. He was giving them the confidence of knowing that the kingdom of God would survive both events. He was encouraging them not to feel too at home in these familiar surroundings anyway, because a new "heaven and earth"—a "new Jerusalem" even—is coming to replace the ones we know (Revelation 21:1-4).

Verse 32. When Jesus said that "this generation"—the one He was talking to at this moment—would "not pass away until all these things are fulfilled," how can that be true? I mean, He hasn't even come again *yet*, much less *then!* That's true. And that's certainly what His followers were thinking—or at least would *come* to think—that Jesus would return before they died (1 Thessalonians 4:17). Since we know Jesus doesn't lie, though, He must have been talking about the fall of Jerusalem, which many of the people listening to Him at this moment *did* see with their own eyes.

21:34-38 Surviving the Fallout

Jesus' parting advice—much the same as it was in 12:35-48—was to be heads-up, on the ball, fully alert, and expecting the Lord's return. He gave specific warnings about "carousing" (literally, "hangovers"), "drunkenness, and worries of life"—anything that might dull our spiritual attention and keep our focus on ourselves. For the believer, Christ's second coming is what we're all living for. Be caught looking up.

Luke then sums up the way Jesus spent His final few days—praying, teaching, preparing . . . waiting.

Luke 22

ISCARIOT.
It's just a last name. It means "man of Kerioth," thought to be a minor city in Judea.

PASSOVER.
This is the opening feast of the seven-day festival called the Feast of Unleavened Bread, commemorating God's deliverance of His people from slavery [see Exodus 12]—when death came to all the firstborn of the Egyptians but "passed over" the people of Israel.

22:1-6 The Plot Is Decided On

The final piece of the kill-Jesus conspiracy came together when Judas showed up in a backroom meeting. Now the Jewish leaders had a point person, a mole in Jesus' inner circle. The charge against Jesus was blasphemy (publicly mocking God's deity, claiming to be God Himself). The capture would be made in secret, so as to avoid a riot, this being Passover season and all, with so many people in town.

Verse 3. How guilty was Judas? Many of the movies about Jesus' life act like Judas was trying to do the right thing but just went about it wrong. Besides, it seems like he was destined to do this (John 17:12). The Old Testament practically calls his name (Psalm 109:6-8), and in this verse the Devil himself is said to be behind the whole deal. Yes, this scene was part of God's plan, all right, but that didn't keep Judas from being a willing participant—a welcome home for Satan to come into and possess. Can the Devil "enter" a person who's trusting in Jesus? Not according to James 4:7, where he was last seen fleeing from those of us who "submit to God" and "resist" the enemy.

22:7-38 The Last Supper Is Served

Passover Preparations (verses 7-13)
Jesus had never been one to go along with nitpicking traditions, but when it came to obeying God's law, He wouldn't let even His impending death keep Him from being faithful to His Father's command. The Passover would go on—even if it had to be at a location kept secret until the last moment from His closest disciples (Judas in particular?). Jesus' prophetic insight showed through in His words to Peter and John, accurately foretelling every last detail of their search for a meeting place, even down to the odd

sight of a man (instead of a woman) carrying water through the streets.

The Lord's Supper (verses 14-20)

Mark this as a key passage of Scripture—the first Lord's Supper, also known as Communion. "When the hour came" (Jesus never did anything haphazardly), He transformed an ancient Jewish practice into a living reminder of His death and the establishment of a "new covenant"—admission into God's family by way of Christ's forgiving blood.

Like Passover, the Lord's Supper was a testimony to divine deliverance, being fulfilled before their eyes in the person of Jesus. Yet its ultimate fulfillment is still waiting for the day when we receive the reward of our salvation and sit down with Him in heaven at the "marriage feast of the Lamb" (Revelation 19:9).

LORD'S SUPPER.
Different churches celebrate this in different ways and believe slightly different things about it, but it's basically a "remembrance" of Christ's death and forgiveness (1 Corinthians 11:23-26).

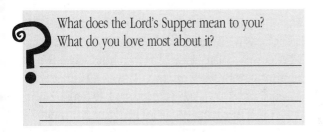

What does the Lord's Supper mean to you? What do you love most about it?

Prelude to a Betrayal (verses 21-23)

We've seen this coming. We can only imagine the look on Judas' face at being found out, or the way Jesus held His human fears in check . . . with His betrayer less than one good lightning bolt away.

Perhaps the strangest aspect is that each of the other disciples—the ones who had nothing at all to do with the blood money or the backhanded scheming—thought maybe the betrayer could be him! (This is clearer in Matthew 26:21-25, where even Judas gives it the "surely not I?" routine.) Each was scared to death because in their hearts they knew there were times they had doubted. Perhaps there's a little Judas in all of us.

TWELVE TRIBES.
These were family lines dating back to the sons of Jacob (Genesis 49:28). Every Jewish person—even up until Jesus' time—was known as coming from one of these families. The "twelve tribes" simply means all the people of Israel.

One Stupid Argument (verses 24-30)

We've been *here* before, too. In one of Jesus' first allusions to His coming suffering (back in 9:44-46), His disciples started fussing over "who would be the greatest" in His kingdom. And here they were—still at it. Jesus didn't seem stern, however. He just patiently reminded them of a truth they couldn't seem to see yet. It was a message we'd heard Him say over and over throughout this Gospel: that the kingdom of God has a whole new set of playing rules. It's not about being great. It's about being a servant . . . and letting God be what's great about us.

These men would learn this—and live this—and die for this. That's why Jesus probably didn't say this in anger but rather commended them just for being there, promising them a reward for their faithfulness.

JESUS' PRAYERS.
One of the things Jesus is doing right now is praying to the Father for you. He "always lives to intercede" for us, to bring our needs before the throne of God (Hebrews 7:25).

Three Denials, Coming Up (verses 31-34)

To read this passage is to understand why we don't deserve what Jesus does for us—and why we should want to be like Him, why His strength of character is so compelling. What power—Satan himself has to run his requests past Jesus for permission. What love—Jesus, on His knees for someone whose own knees are too weak to carry His own promises. What vision—He didn't see Peter the coward of the courtyard but Peter the backbone of the early church. What a great Lord and Friend our Jesus is!

Two Standby Swords (verses 35-38)

Back at the first part of chapters 9 and 10, Jesus had sent His followers out into the nearby villages to announce that a new kingdom was here. It wasn't easy work, but it wasn't life-threatening either. Most people were friendly and receptive. *Well, that was then; this is now!* Jesus was about to be "counted among the outlaws" (a prophecy from Isaiah 53:12)—and so were those who chose to side with Him.

Verse 36. Was Jesus telling His disciples to go out in a blaze of glory, taking as many enemies with them as possible? It hardly seems to add up. In verse 51 He rebuked Peter for doing that very thing. Then Jesus Himself, of course, went on to model what a passive response to suffering looks like. So which approach was He advocating? Most likely it wasn't that He was opposed to their packing a sword to defend themselves. In fact, He pretty much suggested it. But no sword could be as great a weapon as their faith in Him and their trust in His Word (Deuteronomy 33:29).

22:39-71 The Arrest Is Made

A Passionate Prayer (verses 39-46)

Jesus had been spending a lot of time on the Mount of Olives this week (see 21:37). Tonight He had company. Were His disciples worried about Him—or worried about themselves? Who knows? Perhaps they were there half out of loyalty, half out of fear. But they certainly didn't sense the full weight of what was happening up there that night. Not the way *they* were sleeping.

Even in His final hours of freedom, Jesus was teaching His disciples about prayer: that prayer is a key to resisting temptation, that it's hard to be running from God and talking to Him at the same time. But His message must wait for another day before it could finally start sinking into their spirits. For now, Jesus must endure this greatest trial of His life alone, while blood beaded on His forehead, while His Father continued to place our salvation's demands on His innocent back.

GOD'S WILL.
Verse 42 is a go-to passage when people ask you why they don't always get what they pray for. Jesus' pattern is to make bold requests of God—(He did)—but to never close a prayer without realizing that God's will takes precedence over ours, and that His will is what we ultimately want to happen.

A Double-Crossing Kiss (verses 47-53)

The mob that suddenly interrupts Jesus in mid-sentence included the chief priests (the political leadership of the Jewish people), the temple police (law enforcement), elders (respected family heads), plus, as one of the Gospels reports, a detachment of Roman soldiers (John 18:3).

And Judas, of course.

HIGH PRIEST.
In the Old Testament this office was held for life by one of the sons of Aaron, Moses' brother. By New Testament days it had become a Roman practice to appoint someone to the high priesthood in return for political favors.

GALILEAN ACCENT.
Northern folks, who were not so thoroughly Jewish, had a different way of pronouncing the guttural sounds so common in their language.

SANHEDRIN.
The Sanhedrin (san-HE-drin) was the highest Jewish ruling council of the first century, consisting of seventy members plus the high priest. This body had some level of authority under the Roman system of government, but not the power to pass a death sentence (John 18:31).

HONEST HEROES.
One solid defense for the Bible's authenticity is that God chose to present its greatest characters with obvious flaws. If people had been making the Bible up, they would never have included such uncomplimentary stories. The Bible is not a book about great men and women but about a great God working through ordinary people.

It was enough to make quick-tempered Peter want to pull out one of those swords Jesus was talking about in verse 36. But this wasn't a night for the good guys to appear to prevail. For a few more hours Satan and his "dominion of darkness" had God's OK to wreak as much havoc as they could stir up. But they'd better enjoy this "hour" while they had it. It was the last chance the demons would ever get to feel victorious in Jesus' life.

A Night of Denials (verses 54-62)

All of the Gospels record this famous event, but Luke's is the most complete, the most gut-wrenching. You probably already know the story. Peter, numb with fear and blood-curdling dread, stumbled toward the warmth of a courtyard bonfire. News of Jesus' arrest had started to trickle through the milling crowds and travelers. Suddenly Peter was spotted, identified. But he denied knowing anything about Jesus—once, twice, three times.

Then there was Luke's heartbreaking picture—of Jesus turning His head as He was being led toward the trial court, of Peter catching Jesus' eye. (Wonder what the look on Jesus' face said?) Oh, if Peter had "remembered the word of the Lord" before it was too late, before it had found him guilty!

> **?** Peter was Jesus' closest friend and most committed follower, yet he denied Christ three times. How could this have been prevented? What caused him to crack?
>
> _____
> _____
> _____
> _____

A Slap in the Face (verses 63-71)

Even before His trial (if you could call it that), Jesus was already being tortured, made fun of, and prodded into seeing whether He would crack under the strain. Once morning came, the panel of judges basically passed sentence, hearing what they wanted to hear, twisting Jesus' wise words into a confession. Now it was on to the Roman court ... to get what they really wanted ... permission to kill Him!

Luke 23

23:1-25 Jesus' Trial

Jesus Before Pilate (verses 1-5)

The thin charge of blasphemy had stuck in the Sanhedrin, but in the Roman law books this was hardly a crime. So the Jewish leaders trumped up some new charges to try to get a death sentence from Pilate. They said Jesus was "subverting" the nation (being a public nuisance), encouraging tax evasion (defying Roman law), and parading around as a king (posing as a rival to the Roman emperor).

The only thing Pilate wanted discussed was the last charge. And he wanted to hear it from Jesus Himself. But even to a bloodthirsty tyrant like Pilate, who hated the Jews and everything they stood for, Jesus seemed for all the world like an innocent man. I mean—duh!—what had He done? Should Pilate lock Jesus up just for claiming to be a king? I don't know, maybe the emperor (his boss) had given Pilate instructions to lighten up a little. Maybe he was just in a good mood that day. But this Jesus—this so-called "King of the Jews"—just didn't seem like He was causing enough trouble to be a concern.

Don't give Pilate the pass here for trying to be nice, though. Yes, he was trying to play innocent, as though it was all the fault of these people who were pressuring him into making a decision. He was wanting to cast himself in the role of a victim, but he was a feature character in this drama. No matter how hard he washed his hands (Matthew 27:24), he was guilty of Jesus' blood.

Jesus Before Herod (verses 6-12)

Pilate now passed the buck, avoiding a ticklish situation by sending Jesus to someone else for a ruling. But Herod, who had jurisdiction over Jesus' hometown of Nazareth— and who just happened to be in Jerusalem at the time— had about the same reaction to Jesus as Pilate did: amused, but not itching to murder Him.

PILATE.
He became Roman governor over the territory of Judea around A.D. 26. He was known as being bitterly cruel to his Jewish subjects but was eventually removed from office by his Roman superiors.

HEROD.
Herod was the family name of several men who held positions of authority in Palestine (the holy land). This particular one, Herod Antipas, was the same one who killed John the Baptist (Mark 6:14-29) and had toyed before with killing Jesus (13:31).

SUFFERING SERVANT.
Perhaps the clearest prophecy of Jesus' suffering, especially His silence in verse 9, comes from Isaiah 52:13—53:12.

So Herod let his men rough Jesus up a little, seeing if he could twist Jesus' arm into putting on a little miracle sideshow. You can almost see him snickering with his new pal Pilate over what they were going to do with this guy, trying to figure out which was worse—killing an innocent plaything or putting up with this noisy crowd.

So now we have two objective, even hostile rulers who couldn't find anything criminal in Jesus. Luke the historian would want you to mark that down. Jesus was an innocent man.

Pilate's Last Stand? (verses 13-25)

Crawl inside the conscience of Pilate for a second. He had one, you know—just like everybody—an inborn sense of right and wrong. We've already seen him declare Jesus innocent once (verse 4). Now he does it a second time (verse 14), a third time (verse 22), and probably once more in between, if the crowd could have possibly heard him over their shouting (verse 20).

But what *really* rules Pilate? Right and wrong? Or the "pressure" of enough people making enough hard demands? We know the answer to that: "their voices won out." So there you have it—another clear case of poor leadership, of conscience giving way to convenience.

BARABBAS.
Verse 19 tells us nearly all we know about this sideline character from Jesus' trial drama.

Pilate's little bait-and-switch maneuver (verse 17) was a custom he had adopted—probably to ease that conscience of his—where he would release one prisoner of the people's choice during Passover week (Mark 15:6). It was another way for him to dodge having to make a principled decision on Jesus' case. So he was still plenty guilty of Jesus' death, but so was the crowd, who would stand for nothing less (Acts 2:22-24).

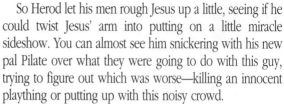

Talk about peer pressure! These people were being needled by their leaders to join the call for Jesus' crucifixion. At what point could you have broken from the crowd and stood in Jesus' corner? How would you have done it?

23:26-32 The Way to the Cross

So justice had failed. An innocent man was being put to death. Some people already knew that—namely, the women who were brave enough to be seen weeping over Jesus in public. Where His disciples were, nobody knows. John alone was the only one ever mentioned as being nearby (John 19:26).

Jesus knew that justice had failed as well. Yet even on the strained walk to His execution, He was able to express compassion for His followers. His words were heavy. He spoke (as He had in chapter 21) about the fall of Jerusalem. For if the Roman authorities could do this now to an innocent man, imagine what they could do later to a nation demanding independence in a Roman-ruled world? Truly, "dry" Jerusalem and its proud tradition were soon to be "cut down and thrown into the fire," just as John the Baptist had said (3:9).

23:33-49 The Crucifixion

Scene of the Crime (verses 33-38)

The Bible leaves out most of the gory details, but trust us—crucifixion was gruesome. First the beating with whips laced with metal and bone, which took most of the life out of the prisoner and kept the soldiers from having to sit around so long waiting for the man to die. Then the burden of carrying your own crossbeam. Then the ropes to secure you in place—or nails (if a quicker death was desired) through the wrists and feet—followed by being lifted into place, naked and exposed, hideously humiliated, left to die by the loss of blood circulation, by coronary failure. Perhaps for days. In Jesus' case, for hours.

But amid the horror, notice something rather special: Jesus fulfilling one prophecy after another. Crucified between thieves (Isaiah 53:12), given "sour wine" to drink (Psalm 69:21), mocked by the onlookers (Psalm 22:7), His clothes divided up and gambled over (Psalm 22:18). This

CYRENIAN.
The city of Cyrene was located in northern Africa. Simon may have been one of the Greek-speaking Jews who lived in Jerusalem during the first century.

HILLS AND MOUNTAINS.
Jesus' words from verse 30 come from another one of those double-exposure prophecies (Hosea 10:8) that warned both of Israel's captivity by the Assyrians in 722 B.C. as well as the fall of Jerusalem in A.D. 70.

GOLGOTHA.
Also known as "the Skull," this craggy mountainside outside of Jerusalem sort of looks like a skeletal human head—the nose, the eye sockets. It may have been called this, though, simply because it was used as a place of death, a place of skulls. Its Latin name, which became our word "Calvary," also means "skull."

true Passover Lamb was being slain under a handwritten sign more true than His executioners knew. They weren't really killing Him. He was "laying down" His life that He might "take it up again" (John 10:17-18).

A Deathbed Conversion (verses 39-43)

Is there any such thing as a deathbed confession? Yes. You're looking at one. From all we know, these two criminals were guilty of the same or similar crimes. They were alike in many respects. But one of them went to his grave cursing, another believing.

How is that so? It's by grace alone. By simple faith. As easy as falling off a log, yet so hard that many people go to hell unwilling to repent and receive God's mercy.

But for those who receive the revelation of who Jesus is and accept His forgiveness and salvation, a great reward awaits them on the other side. Life in paradise. Life forever. Life with Him—no matter what their life was like up until that time.

Jesus Is Dead (verses 44-49)

It was noon now. But it looked and felt like midnight. The Father had turned His face away (Matthew 27:46)—not from His Son's deity, but from His Son's humanity. Jesus the man must die alone. It was the only way. The curtain that only parted once a year for the high priest to enter, bearing a sacrifice of blood for his own sins as well as for the sins of the people, was now miraculously sliced "down the middle." Jesus, the great high priest, had "entered the holy of holies once for all" with His own precious blood . . . to pay for the sins of His people now and forevermore (Hebrews 9:11-14).

Hallelujah!

At the time, though, it certainly didn't seem so good. Those who knew Him were standing "at a distance" in shock and disbelief. Even those who had called for His crucifixion were scared silly, cowering toward home, wishing they could somehow get away from themselves.

But even in the midst of this horrible event, some sensed

ON TO HEAVEN?
We mentioned this at the story of the rich man and Lazarus [16:19-31], but here's another example that when we die, we go immediately into "paradise" with Jesus. No waiting room, no sleeplike existence. We close our eyes one moment, then open them in Jesus' presence.

that they had witnessed more than the death of an ordinary man. The centurion would not be the last Gentile (non-Jew), nor would Joseph (in the next passage) be the last Jew, to find himself swept into God's kingdom through belief in Jesus Christ.

23:50-56 The Burial of Jesus

The reason Luke and the other Gospel writers included this event in their writings was to make sure everybody was clear on this fact: Jesus actually died. Why is this so important? Because some people believe He just sort of passed out or "swooned," then regained consciousness again in the cool air of the tomb and slipped out. (Pretty big rock to move, though, for a guy who's been beat to a pulp and left hanging by His hands for six hours!)

CENTURION.
A Roman officer, usually a career soldier, who commanded about one hundred men ("cent-" is a prefix meaning 100).

PROPITIATION.
Big word (pro-PITCH-ee-AY-shun) to explain why Jesus' death matters. In Old Testament times a sacrifice was required to appease God's wrath. Yet the people's sin wasn't really eliminated, only covered. Jesus, though, who lived a perfect human life (which no fallen person could have done, only God) was made "to be sin for us" (2 Corinthians 5:21). He carried our sin "in His body" to the cross (1 Peter 2:24). So God is not just giving us the pass when He saves us. He is justified in declaring us innocent, because Jesus has become our substitute, our "propitiation" (1 John 4:10).

Verse 56. One big question is this: what was Jesus doing during this down time between His death and His resurrection? Some believe, primarily from 1 Peter 3:18-20, that He went into hell to preach salvation to the already dead. That may be. But the phrase He spoke to the thief on the cross—"Today you will be with Me in paradise"—seems to indicate that He went immediately into heaven and the Father's presence. It's a difficult thing to understand and impossible to know for sure.

But for those left behind, it was a sick-to-their-stomach Saturday. A Sabbath even quieter than usual. But what else could they do? The Sabbath must be observed, like always. Life must go on without Him.

Right?

24:1-12 Where Is He?

WOMEN WITNESSES.
Mary Magdalene was a Jesus follower who had been delivered from seven demons [8:2]. Joanna was another He had healed [also 8:2]. The other Mary had ministered to Him in Galilee and was perhaps the mother of one of His disciples, James the son of Alphaeus [Mark 15:40-41].

TWO ANGELS.
Like at the empty tomb, a pair of angels had presided over some of the Bible's most special, holy places. At least two angels stood at the entrance to the garden of Eden [Genesis 3:24], and two angel figures also appeared together above the ark of the covenant [Exodus 25:22].

This is Luke the historian writing. Reporting the facts: Jesus was killed on Friday. Dead all day long on Saturday. Until sometime Sunday morning. And now . . . there's an open door where a large boulder used to be. And a growing field of credible eyewitnesses that show up in this chapter from all corners.

These facts are important, because some would later say: (1) Jesus' body was stolen by His disciples; or (2) the people who saw Him alive again were just hallucinating; or (3) the women who arrived on Sunday morning showed up at the wrong tomb. These are three false ideas among many.

Well, if the first claim is right, then why were those accused of stealing Him (like Peter) so shocked to find that He was gone? In response to the second explanation, how could so many people be dreaming the same thing? And to counteract the third, Luke's already said that the women "observed the tomb and how His body was placed" the day He died (23:55). Besides, if *they* were in the wrong place, so were the two angels, who must have made a wrong turn at Mars or something.

Jesus had been right about every one of His prophecies. How could He be wrong on this most important one?

> **?** Even though the women had heard Jesus speak of His resurrection before, they were still shocked at the news. Did this show a lack of faith on their part? How do you think you would have responded?
>
> _____
>
> _____
>
> _____

24:13-35 Was That Who I Thought It Was?

Luke is the only Gospel writer who included this interesting story—of two guys walking side-by-side with the risen Christ . . . and not even knowing it! As unexpected as the story is, it's still pretty self-explanatory. The thing you wonder most about is: why didn't they recognize Jesus to begin with?

Did He look different than He had before His death? Possibly. Jesus had been raised with a new, resurrected body, one that showed no sign of wear or aging. Have you ever noticed how different a U.S. president looks after four years in office—the gray hair, the lined face? Surely the emotional strain of Jesus' life had taken some toll on His appearance along the way. We know, at least, that the rigors of His death had made Him unrecognizable (Isaiah 53:3-4).

But in this story, His health and vitality had been renewed. He must have looked stronger, more vigorous. He certainly looked human. We know that. The two guys wouldn't have interacted so matter-of-factly with Him if He had been some kind of phantom.

More than anything, though, God was in control of the whole situation (as always), opening the men's eyes to Christ's reality when He knew it was time for them to see.

EMMAUS.
No one's really sure where the town of Emmaus was, except that the Bible says it was "about seven miles from Jerusalem." The word itself means "hot baths."

THE RESURRECTION.
The longest biblical explanation for the importance of Christ's resurrection is found in 1 Corinthians 15:12-58.

24:36-43 Could It Possibly Be?

The same two men from the previous passage were now at the disciples' doorstep, trying hard to put their unbelievable news into words. Then suddenly—somehow—Jesus was there! His request for them to look into His eyes, tap Him on the shoulder, even offer Him something to eat were all opportunities to prove that He was real, not a ghost, not a figment of their imagination. The historian Luke built an iron-clad case for the resurrection of Christ.

24:44-49 What Do We Do Now?

As in verse 7, when the angels at the tomb were explaining to the women why Jesus was no longer there, Jesus Himself reminded His closest followers what He had been telling them all along—in 9:22, in 9:44, in 18:31-33—over and over again—that His suffering and death would be the way to fulfill all prophecy. It would be the way to prove His authority and deity. It would be the way to bring eternal life to His people.

It wasn't that He didn't do a good enough job of teaching them beforehand. Remember, His sayings had been "hidden from them" (18:34) at the time. But this reminder of His earlier predictions was now doing exactly what He wanted—deepening His disciple's faith in Him, anchoring their trust in God's Word, enabling them to possess a trust strong enough to endure when He was no longer there in person.

He had sent them out before (chapters 9 and 10) to proclaim His kingdom. At that time they sort of knew (maybe) what they were talking about. But now they've got the knowledge and understanding to go out there with a passion—proclaiming the good news of Jesus, preaching repentance and forgiveness of sins, just talking about all the things they'd seen and heard.

ACTS.
Remember that Luke is also the author of the book of Acts, which is almost like "volume two"—the sequel to this historical Gospel. So to see what happens next, including the breakout of the Holy Spirit in the disciples' hearts, turn to Acts, chapter 1 ... and continue the story.

24:50-53 You Must Go On

This incredible moment was also captured in Acts 1:9-11 as the link between this Gospel story and the next-chapter story of the early church. This is a scene of awe and worship and probably of some sadness at saying goodbye again. But their only response to seeing Jesus in all His power and glory was to obey—to go back to Jerusalem like He'd told them to (verse 49), to wait for the coming of the Holy Spirit.

We leave His followers at the end of Luke, praising Him. And we leave our own study of His amazing life story, praising Him.

"Continually."

What amazes you the most about Jesus' life? What aspect of *your* life will never be the same again after being this "up close" with Him? What are some things Jesus said that you'll never, ever forget?

_____

_____

_____

_____

_____

_____

_____

_____

_____

_____

_____

_____

_____

_____

_____

_____

_____

_____

_____

_____

_____

_____

_____

_____

_____

_____

WHERE'S JESUS?

He was "carried up into heaven," where He still lives today— not as He was before coming to earth as a baby, but always bearing the image of His humanity, always bearing the scars of His crucifixion, "always able to save those who come to God through Him, since He always lives to intercede for them" (Hebrews 7:25).

If you liked "UP CLOSE WITH JESUS"
(Getting Deep in the Book of Luke) . . .
Check out these other TruthQuest Commentaries:

CHRISTIAN TO THE CORE
Getting Deep in the Book of James
ISBN 0-8054-2853-4

A LIFE AND DEATH EXPERIENCE
Getting Deep in the Book of Romans
ISBN 0-8054-2857-7
(available September 2004)

NEVER SAY DIE
Getting Deep in the Book of Revelation
ISBN 0-8054-2854-2
(available September 2004)